*Praying
Your
Story*

Praying Your Story

Making Sense of Your Life Through
Fables, Prayers and the Company of Saints

William Cleary

illustrated by Maureen Noonan

FOREST OF PEACE
Publishing

Suppliers for the Spiritual Pilgrim
Leavenworth, KS

Also by William Cleary

Prayers and Fables
How the Wild Things Pray
The Lively Garden Prayer Book
Lighten Your Heart
Prayers for Lovers
Prayers to She Who Is
A Doubter's Prayerbook

Centering Prayers
Facing God
Churchmouse Tales from the Vatican
Hyphenated Priests *(edited)*
Selving *(edited)*
Psalm Services for Group Prayer
Psalm Services for Church Meetings

Praying Your Story

copyright © 2002, by William Cleary

Library of Congress Cataloging-in-Publication Data

Cleary, William.
    Praying your story : making sense of your life through fables, prayers, and the company of saints / William Cleary.
        p. cm.
    Chiefly 40 rhyming verses of Aesop's fables.
    Includes index.
    ISBN 0-939516-57-8 (pbk.)
        1. Meditations .   2. Aesop's fables—Adaptations.   3. Christian saints—Prayer-books and devotions—English. 4. Fables, Greek—Adaptations. I. Aesop's fables. II. Title.

    BV4832.3 .C57   2002
    242—dc21   2001054529

published by

Forest of Peace Publishing, Inc.
PO Box 269
Leavenworth, KS 66048-0269   USA
1-800-659-3227
www.forestofpeace.com

printed by

Hall Commercial Printing
Topeka, KS 66608-0007

1st printing: January 2002

illustrations by

Maureen Noonan

Dedication

for Tom and Neil
beloved chapters in the fable of my life

Note
The forty rhyming verses of Aesop's fables in this book are of my own invention and choice. Forty others appear in the 1998 book *Prayers and Fables: Meditating on Aesop's Wisdom* from Sheed and Ward. These eighty fables seemed the most engaging among the 358 fables in *Aesop: The Complete Fable*s (Penguin, 1998). —*William Cleary*

Table of Contents

III. God Helps Those Who Help Themselves

IV. We Often Are Our Own Worst Enemies

V. The Wise Avoid Foolish Expectations

About the Saints in *Praying Your Story*

Theologian Elizabeth Johnson has most recently renewed and inspired our interest in "saints." I place that word in quotation marks because many people are saints to us who are as yet not canonized, not yet earning the title Saint, with a capital S. Johnson's 1998 book *Friends of God and Prophets* is a thorough renewal of the theology of the Communion of Saints and a call, as well, to include in our rituals memories of and prayers to those many others (especially holy women who are rather poorly represented in our official canon of Saints) who deserve our reverence. Even in the immensely popular and brilliantly written *All Saints* by Robert Ellsberg there is an imbalance of men (284) to women (81). The saints in *Praying Your Story* come mostly from Ellsberg, but also other sources, and give attention to some important women not included in Ellsberg.

What really matters is what Johnson recommends in the introduction to her book: that we begin to explore a relationship to our holy departed which is not based on the metaphors of the medieval court — where in the old days saints might be asked to intercede for us with the royalty (God, Christ, Mary), presuming that the saints have influence on the "powers that be" which we don't have.

Johnson suggests an entirely different reason for praying to the saints: just to communicate with them. Our prayer can allow us just to have a moment to remember them reverently and to remind them — if they can hear us, and most of us feel instinctively that they can — of our love for them, of our admiration for them, of how they inspire us, and of our anticipation that when we die, we shall join their company — in the "great cloud of witnesses" spoken of by St. Paul.

So the prayers in this book do not include the commonplace petition: "Pray for us." Our usual phrase is "Be with us," "You inspire us," and "We admire you." Invoking their holy memory is to refuse to let them, in their death, be erased from history. Instead, in addition to giving them their place in history, we make them a part of our own history, finding in their lives a modeling for our own life stories. Because they have shown bravery and insight, trust and patience in adversity, we are emboldened to think we can do the same, strengthened by common membership in the communion of saints.

Introduction

Do you wonder at times if your life has meaning? Does it add up to anything? Or is it "a tale told by an idiot, full of sound and fury, signifying nothing"?

Another way to put this: Is your life a story? A fable perhaps? Does it have, like Aesop's, a moral?

My friend, novelist Michael Davidson, once sent a messenger from God to earth with the astonishing revelation: "randomness is order squared." He meant that when we add up the events of any human life, they may appear to have no organization, to be meaningless, as pointless as a random number — like 11,843,936. Apparently — to the naked eye — absurd, signifying nothing. But they aren't. 11,843,936 is, in fact, 3456 squared. There is order beneath the randomness. So, metaphorically, Davidson's messenger from God taught that if you just get the right perspective, you can make sense of everything.

But what is it that makes such a message, such a theology, plausible?

First of all, it is not plausible without a leap of faith. Yet the evidence of meaning and promise and intelligent design in a morning sunrise, a child's laughter, a father's caringness, a mother's protective instincts — is quite compelling. Right there you leap, or, as Chesterton said, you vote: You vote for the world. You affirm it. It's a choice, a leap — of faith. If part of the world contains meaning, the whole must have meaning — just as apples are evidence of apple trees somewhere.

Secondly, our own personal story presents a similar challenge. Is it a meaningful progression of a beginning, a middle and an end? This present book suggests it is. We can't see the meaning of everything that happens. Still, we affirm in advance that it is — for all its apparent absurdity — meaningful. We need not say that everything that happens is "the will of God" but rather that God can bring meaning out of whatever happens. Everything is "the way of God." A death, for instance, often seems to make no sense. Yet if we affirm it, if we accept it as a functional part of a natural life — if it is, for instance, "going home," the end of a story — it makes sense. Perspective is everything.

Aesop's remarkable fables are at this book's heart. Aesop was probably African — we suspect that because the animals in his fables are African. He was apparently captured and taken forcibly to Greece some 2,500 years ago. There he told hundreds of wisdom-bearing stories that were never forgotten. Centuries later Plutarch listed him as one of history's seven wisest men. To the wisdom of Aesop this book adds a contemplative, often offbeat, prayer that testifies to our contemporary preoccupations: Are we also, like timid bunnies, too fearful? Are we foolish lovers? Are we egocentric? We pray to improve, to live with faith in and vision into life's meaningfulness.

And finally, we turn to the heroines and heroes of our own time, the "saints," in whose spiritual company Judeo-Christians have been taught to live their lives — and newly taught since the advent of Elizabeth Johnson's feminist theology of the Communion of Saints. Johnson says: "[The Communion of Saints is a doctrine] so . . . relational, so intrinsically inclusive and egalitarian, so respectful of persons who are defeated and praising of those who succeed against all odds, so hope-filled and so pragmatic, [it] has the potential to empower all those who struggle for human dignity in the name of God."

But the dominant paradigm of all this is story. Nothing so powerfully unifies the spirituality of modern believers as the concept of story, honoring our own experience and telling our own story as we join in a circle of faith. Listening to the stories of others is a bonding process. We come to belong to each other. Thus is created community, and out of that comes strength, our personal strength to carry on, and our community's strength to believe that together progress, reverence for diversity and a civil human life is possible for us.

Finally, into our own circle we must bring the saints — and that includes all those we know as well as those who have lived throughout history. Their lives are fables like our own, and while they may have gone down to death without understanding why or seeing the meaningfulness of it all, from our perspective some of the meaning and beauty has become visible. We can see how what they did was "fabulous" and how they can companion us in our own time. Thus, I have joined some saint from the recent or distant past to each of the forty meditations, with the hope that we will find inspiration in their lives for our own trials and frustrations. Says Johnson: ". . . Remembrance of forebears in the faith enhances self-identity, releasing a power to go forward in their spirit and with their unfinished agendas."

In the end, the only imaginable way that God can bring good out of some of the horrors in human life is in a life after death. Without it, much of life would be undeniably absurd, unjust and irrational — the conviction of many people today, in fact. A life after death is, for them, a gratuitous superstition. Yet even scientific minds can be open to a faith that carries one beyond provable conclusions. "Nothing is too wonderful to exist": This line from scientist Michael Faraday stands emblazoned across the lintel of the Department of Science at the University of California in Berkeley. A continuation of life after death may seem to some "too wonderful to exist," but nothing in science makes it impossible, and everything in human experience makes it plausible. In fact, the more unfair and nonsensical and absurd an event is, the more it trumpets the necessity of another world where "every tear is wiped away."

With this attitude, we can, with our saint Dag Hammarskjöld (page 81), say "thanks" for all that has been and "yes" to all that will be — as he suggested in his classic book *Markings*. Thus we can in faith rejoice in the past, trusting in the Creative Mystery, God, to give it full meaning, value and triumph. Then in faith we can even befriend the future, and without arrogance or presumption say in prayer: Yes. Yes, let it happen. Let it come about. I refuse to ultimately fear it. I may fear much about it: the pain, the failures, the losses, the unknown. But on balance I rejoice in much about it: the new life each day, the achievements, the loves discovered and lived. What will happen, no one (perhaps not even God) knows. But whatever that is: Yes.

William Cleary
Winter 2001

Part I

Follow Your Faith
and Not Your Fears

1. Some Timid Bunnies Change Their Tune

One day some bunnies gathered round
To moan their awful fate.
They cried: *How sad it is to live*
With terrors small and great,
Those hunters, dogs and wolves we dread!
That is no life! We're better dead!

Let's die! said they, and headed down
Into a pond to crash,
But as they galloped toward the pond,
They heard an awful SPLASH!
About a thousand frightened frogs
Had thought they were attacked by dogs!

Stop! said one bunny. *Don't you see*
How dumb is all this fuss?
These frogs have more to fear than we!
They're even scared of us!
It's not our fate we should despise.
It is our fear! That's what's unwise!

***Moral:* Follow your faith and**
not your fears.

PRAYER to befriend the cosmos

Holy Creative Mystery,
the words of humans cannot begin to utter enough gratitude
just to be alive, to be, and to be here, now,
at the end of an almost infinite chain of cosmic events
that made it possible for us to breathe and think
and see,
amidst an unspeakably complex world —
honored to have been born into the circle of living things,
into the elemental family of matter and energy,
part of the dance that whirls about the sun,
a functioning segment of the mysterious cosmos,
and destined, we trust, for a no less complex and wonderful future.
We need not fear: We are in loving hands.
Immense and magnetic as our universe is,
ancient as are its beginnings, complex as are its parts,
yet our hearts' longings are still more immense and magnetized.
They find your own mystery, Holy One, steadily attractive.
So today we simply let ourselves go:
toward you, into your mystery,
trusting that the world's astonishing order
signifies intelligibility
and caringness
beneath all of its mysteries. Amen.

Praying Your Story

Recall the luckiest thing that ever happened to you. Of course you were surprised by it. Does not God have innumerable surprises ahead for us? Give thanks.

Follow your faith and not your fears.

PRAYER to John XXIII, beloved contemporary pope

. . . for courageous optimism

Good Pope John the Twenty-Third,
history-making leader and irrepressible optimist:
Give us all faith in ourselves, and in God,
ignoring all "prophets of doom" as you called them.
Though already in old age when elected pope,
you took on the momentous Second Vatican Council, and declared:
"We are not on earth to guard a museum,
but to cultivate a flourishing garden of life."
Thus your courage liberated us from an obsolete past,
and seeded a garden of reforms unheard of in church history.
Model for us faith in ourselves and readiness for risk.
Amen.

It often happens that I wake at night and begin to think about a serious problem and decide I must tell the Pope about it. Then I wake up completely and remember that I am the Pope.

—Pope John XXIII

Biographical Note

A Pope Everyone Loved   Angelo Giuseppe Roncalli (1881–1963) was the child of an Italian peasant family, brought up a church diplomat and elected pope at age 77. Only three months after his election, he announced an ecumenical council, but died long before it ended. His generous approach to religion deeply affected the church and the whole world. He cared passionately for the rights of all humans, and firmly placed the church on the side of the oppressed everywhere. He was beatified in September of 2000.

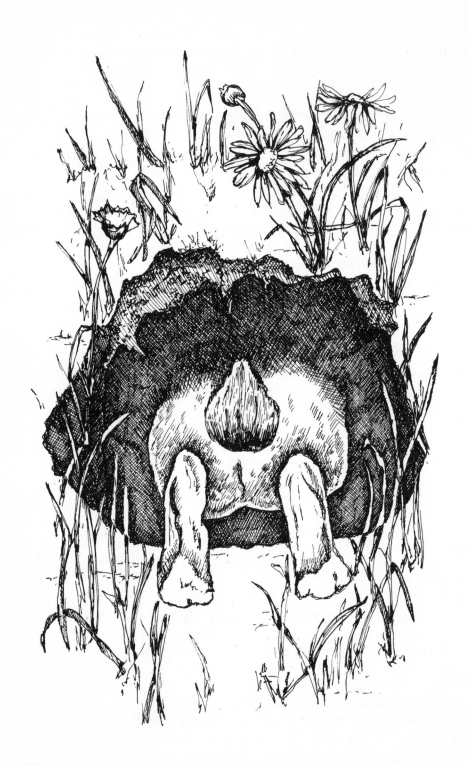

2. The Hare Outruns a Hound

There once was a hound who discovered a hare
    In the woods on the top of a knoll.
He barked in delight and gave chase till the night
    But the hare disappeared down a hole.

What a laugh! mocked a shepherd, *Can't you be more quick*
    Hunting food for your puppies and wife?
Answered Hound: *Friend, it's one thing to run for your lunch —*
    Another to run for your LIFE!

Moral: **Your needs often decide your performance.**

PRAYER to slow down

It comforts me, Holy God outside of time,
to realize that you are time's inventor —
so you have total grasp of the disciplines of living in time:
not to give our life either an unnatural pace
or too slow a tempo,
not to miss opportunities,
not to come late, not to run out of time,
anxieties all too common in our world.
Often we speak to you as if you too were time-bound —
though you aren't.
Instead, you live outside of time,
in that land we glimpse just occasionally,
in ecstasy or delight,
a land to which we travel
not by hurrying up but by slowing down.
Guide us there often.
Amen.

Praying Your Story

Remember a time in your life when you surprised people by what
you achieved? Were you not highly motivated? If you took a longer
perspective on your life, might you not achieve more?

Your needs often decide your performance.

PRAYER to Catherine of Siena, dynamic medieval woman

. . . for energetic serenity

Holy Catherine, who died long centuries ago,
fiery doctor of the church in wild times,
never will history erase the memory of your triumphs of energy,
of mediation and mysticism in a mere 33 years of life,
famed for quick work but total focus.
Like you and with your companionship, we will honor contemplation,
but also join in the struggles of our own times:
Yours were shameful warring churchmen and the disastrous Black Death;
ours are the global oppression of women, AIDS
and looming environmental disaster.
As you labored, Catherine, with such signal success,
believing in God's loving support,
so, be with us in all our crises today.
Like you, we will not deny our own imagination's visions and voices,
nor lose hope that our race, with the help of God,
will be able to survive its challenges.
Amen.

My convent cell will not be one of stone or wood, but of self-knowledge.
—Catherine of Siena

Biographical Note

A Woman Unique in History Declared, in 1970, a Doctor of the Church, Catherine of Siena (1347-1380) is one of the most influential women in Christian history. Daughter of a prosperous man (she was twenty-fourth of twenty-five children), she developed early as a kind of volcano of energy and persuasive intelligence. She also had the ability to envision the spiritual world, and felt she could converse with Christ and the saints. She mediated disputes, solved problems between nations, and once even persuaded the Pope to move out of France and back to Rome. She wrote an important mystical work, her *Dialogue*, and filled her short life with accomplishments of both action and contemplation.

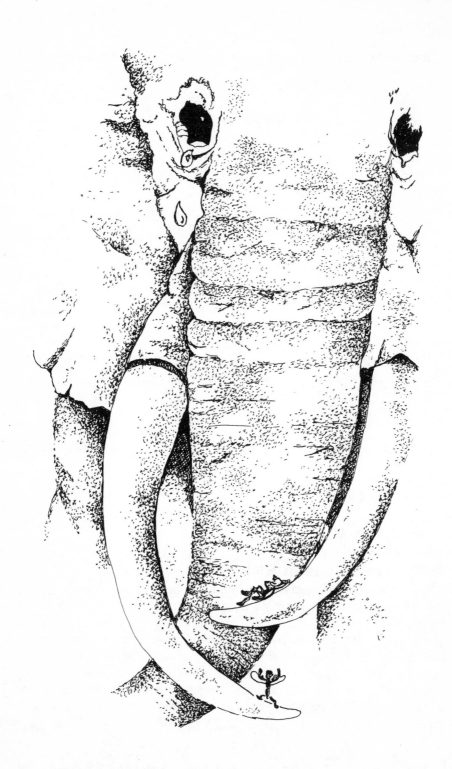

3. The Lion Is Ashamed To Feel Afraid

I'm just so embarrassed, a lion once mused,
To jump when a cock cockadoodle-dee-doos.
> *Great Jupiter, help out this poor ignoramus!*
> *Where is that great courage that makes lions famous?*

So Jupiter took him along for a joke
To the home of an elephant tall as an oak.
They called into one of his dark habitats,
> *Go away!* came a voice, *I'm hiding from GNATS!*

> *They fly round my head, they buzz in my ears.*
> *They first make me cry and then swim in my tears.*
> *They fly up my trunk and they chew on my soul!*
> *They might kill me! I can't even go for a stroll!*

How lion did laugh at the cries of the brute,
So much larger than he but more frightened, to boot!
Then Jupiter led lion back to his lair,
Where roosters still scared him, but he didn't care.

Moral: **Even the great have
foolish fears.**

PRAYER to see a molehill in every mountain

My God, Sunlight in which I am bathed, Ocean of love,
Mystery beyond naming,
I feel the reality of your hidden being
drawing me along my road of destiny and truest selfhood,
and I lift up my eyes today to the larger realities,
perspectives I seldom see unless I pause to do so:
the deep goodness of simply existing,
the breathtaking canyon
of what's wonderfully unfathomable in this creation,
the caringness of good order
that has surrounded many of us from our earliest days,
the sacraments of friendship and family.
In the perspective of this fuller reality,
the occasionally uphill terrain of my life's path
often shrinks to molehill proportions.
What I foolishly fear becomes manageable,
and I learn to see my life in context,
in perspective,
and with the eyes of the accumulated wisdom of the ages.
Amen.

Praying Your Story

Have you found yourself fearing things too much? Can you remember any time when you were laughably afraid of something insignificant? Recall the details in God's presence.

Even the great have foolish fears.

PRAYER to Henri Nouwen, modernday prophet

. . . for faithfulness

Wounded healer, brother Henri,
now at last you are at peace, your life remembered, no doubt,
as a storm of anxiety and searching, and a final blessed landfall with God.
Your terrible choices shout the Gospel from the mountaintops:
God is good, the poor are blessed, Jesus lives, his yoke is sweet.
When you finally collapsed in emotional breakdown and loneliness,
still you kept faith with your creative gifts
and shared in books your anguished wisdom.
Be with us in our own woundedness.
Help us to persevere in faith
and to live in solidarity with the least of God's children.
Amen.

*There is no certainty that my life will be any easier in the years ahead,
or that my heart will be any calmer. But there is the certainty that you
are waiting for me and will welcome me home when I have persevered
in my long journey to your house.*

—Henri Nouwen

Biographical Note

A Guru For Our Time The renowned author of best-selling religious
books like *Wounded Healer* and *Reaching Out* died unexpectedly at age 64,
leaving behind disciples all over the earth. From Catholic priest and university
professor to caretaker of the handicapped, Nouwen (1932-1996) invented for
himself a unique life and teaching, and drew crowds wherever he went,
participating in public life whenever it helped the needy.

4. A Grandma Ewe Saves Her Life

An old grandmother ewe one day
Was sure she would explode
      In terror as she watched a wolf
      Come ambling down her road.

She froze in fear, she could not speak,
She thought she was undone!
      But wolf did not feel hungry so
      He thought he'd just have fun.

Hey, Grandma, would you save your life?
He said, *Come clean with me:*
      Tell me three feelings that you have
      When noble wolves you see.

So grandma said, *Well, honestly,*
One feeling that comes through
      Is loathing that there are such brutes
      As hideous as you.

And second, I'd feel good if wolves
Were quickly all struck blind!
      Then third . . . were slaughtered one and all
      For bullying our kind.

The wolf could not believe his ears
To hear things so UNCOUTH,
      But had to let that grandma go
      Because she'd told the truth.

Moral: **Speaking the truth can work wonders.**

PRAYER to occasionally utter the unvarnished truth

When I speak to you, most awesome loving Mystery —
or rather whom, in faith, I trust is loving —
I am bewildered (to be honest):
so many parts of your creation seem unloving:
volcanoes, hurricanes, tornadoes, birth defects, accidents,
gruesome diseases, inimical animals and murderous insects.
But of one thing I am certain when I speak to you:
You hear the unvarnished truth from me —
for I am aware of your necessarily all-penetrating knowledge
of everything you hold in existence.
You know my heart.
In place of prayer, you hear me say at times simply:
Look! Behold, my soul!
There, plain as day, are all the unvarnished facts of my life,
reaching out to you through the silence.
Hear my heart.
Amen.

Praying Your Story

Recall a time when you admitted to a point of view that was unpopular
and that might have angered others. Do you regret what you did?
Does God share that evaluation?

Speaking the truth can work wonders.

PRAYER to the Syrophoenician Woman,

. . . for fearless perseverance

Passionate unnamed woman of Mark's Gospel,
a dishonored outsider daring to ask a favor
of that busy rabbi and healer, Jesus of Nazareth,
then rebuffed by his words (since she was not a Jew)
"It is not right to take the children's bread
and throw it to the dogs," he said (with a smile on his face?).
How we admire you, Holy Outsider!
Your sick daughter meant everything,
and you persisted in your honest prayer, saying:
". . . even the dogs under the table eat the children's crumbs!"
Thus you ended up with more than crumbs:
Your precious daughter was healed.
And ever since, the Gospel of Jesus is healed of elitism —
which makes you one of the founding "foremothers" of the gentile church.
Companion us all in honest prayer,
and teach us "to use the power we have
in the service of what we say we believe" (Audre Lorde).
Amen.

Change occurs in women's consciousness when they become aware of the contrast between their own human worth and the subordinate status they are assigned by patriarchal systems in public and private realms.
—Elizabeth Johnson

Biographical Note

One Incident Made Her Forever Famous In the seventh chapter of Mark's Gospel this courageous woman appears, and the story of her persistence and fearless advocacy for her sick daughter has never been forgotten. It is said to have shattered the parochialism of Jesus himself. Since she was a gentile, not a Jew, Jesus refuses at first to hear of her needs, but her faith "converts" him to a wider view. Her devotion equaled that of any of his disciples, and she was rewarded for it, becoming a model follower of Jesus for all time.

5. A Fool Scolds a Drowning Child

One day a youngster went to swim
And got swept down the stream,
So she began to shout for help,
But heard a man blaspheme.

> *You god-forsaken backward kid!*
> He cried, *You silly fool,*
> *Why are you there? You're almost drowned!*
> *What have you learned in school?*

He climbed up on a riverbank
To get a better view,
And put his hands upon his hips
And shook his finger too.

> *Kind sir,* she cried, *Yes, I was dumb*
> *To get into this hole,*
> *But show you're wise and SAVE MY LIFE*
> *Before you fix my soul.*

***Moral:* Give care before you
give advice.**

PRAYER for healing from the itch to give advice

Why do you give us so much freedom,
and leave us with so little advice,
Holy Intelligence, Holy Wisdom?
"You spoke and it — the world — was created": I can imagine that.
But you might have added a few "Operating Instructions"
or something on "Troubleshooting."
The Hebrew Writings are addressed mostly to Hebrews,
and the Christian Scripture is far too often vague and ambiguous.
Was all this freedom a calculated risk —
and a lesson to us in how to mentor others (in freedom)?
Yet we find it so hard to let freedom and risk do their work,
not to take over our children's lives
or the governance of foreign peoples,
not to give unasked-for advice,
and not to put sermonizing ahead of compassion.
Give us the wisdom to let freedom have its way with others,
and to use our own with appreciation.
Amen.

Praying Your Story

Have you ever given advice that was resented? Why do we volunteer
so quickly to make decisions for other people? Is not God at times
a model of entrusting imperfect people with big decisions?

Give care before you give advice.

PRAYER to Maura Clark and Companions, murdered in El Salvador

. . . to be faithful to the oppressed

Heroic hearts, loving hearts, Maura, Ita, Dorothy, Jean,
we are honored to call your holy names,
martyrs in our own time, martyrs of compassion.
You could not imagine going to safety when those you loved could not,
risking the same fate as Bishop Romero,
martyred there less than a year before,
unable, like him, to abandon your people,
to exercise your freedom to remain "present"
despite the advice of so many.
Thus you testified to your faith in a God of faithfulness,
enduring the label of "subversive" like your original hero, Jesus of Nazareth.
You fill us with energy,
and the will to be now — as you shall be forever — *"presente"*!
Amen.

Several times I have decided to leave — I almost could, except for the children, the poor bruised victims of adult lunacy. Who would care for them...?

—Jean Donovan

Biographical Note

A Story of an Unforgettable Foursome In late 1980, Sister Maura Clark and fellow Maryknoller Ita Ford, Ursuline Sister Dorothy Kazel and lay volunteer Jean Donovan found themselves in El Salvador, not to prove anything, but because they knew they were needed. Death threats had multiplied against them. The military reign of terror had crushed all appeals for justice and democracy, and thousands had been murdered. Still they remained at their posts, testifying to an unmistakable message of compassion for the oppressed. They were raped and murdered on December 2, 1980.

6. The Wolf Fails To Deceive the Horse

A tricky old wolf once entered a farm,
And seeing oats growing, he put on his charm.
So, calmly pretending that he meant no harm,
      He spoke to a horse in his stall.
Sir Horse, I do hope you are comfortably fed,
But in case you are hungry and famished instead,
There are oats by the ton in one field, he said,
      And I ate none so you'd have all.

Now the horse knew quite well that the wolf hated oats
And cared nothing for horses — or cattle or goats,
And in fact was well known for attacking their throats,
      So he couldn't resist ridicule:

Sir Wolf, he said, *Don't think me over-suspicious*
Were I to suspect there was something malicious
In your lying claim you find oats delicious.
      BEGONE! Do you think me a fool?

***Moral:* Before you believe,
consider the source.**

PRAYER to stand sovereign when I must

Teach me, Holy Sophia, not to avoid that inner honesty
that leaves me bewildered and alone,
that radical questioning of convention
where I lose the comfort of familiar places
and wander in solitary agony,
asking myself: Am I being honest?
Is it wise to trust my own instincts?
Or am I abandoned by grace?
Have I sinned against the light so it is now denied me?
No, I will stand by my inner wisdom,
trust my good native sense and take the consequences.
How I must live is not the imperative of anyone else,
nor can I judge others.
Ultimately I must stand up for what I feel to be true,
true, at least, for me,
remaining open to communal wisdom
but not choosing the comfort of it.
At some inward crossroads, I am a sovereign self, or I am nothing.
There in the half light I must stand my full self,
my only self,
to endure the chilling atmosphere
that sets my heart and mind aglow
where I know a born-again selfhood
green and lively as truth.
Amen.

Praying Your Story

What was the most outlandish thing you ever believed? Is it possible
that at this moment you believe something comparably implausible?
Can God not enlighten the mind?

Before you believe, consider the source.

PRAYER to Emily Dickinson, American poet of the 1800s

. . . to become a sovereign self

There is no way, seraphic Emily Dickinson,
that we can invent a prayer worthy of you —
except inasmuch as we will be plain and direct,
and not try to mimic the rhapsodic angel of inspiration
that you were in your time, though theologically a radical
and a thorough — if lighthearted — non-conformist.
Only in retrospect do we see how colossally successful
was your quiet, reclusive life of only fifty-six short years,
producing 1700 poems.
From you we learn to withhold judgment of anyone's life,
including our own.
Only God's — and history's — final view of it is valid.
As you, Emily, lived out your passionate rebellion
against your culture's expectations
and clung to your own creative vision,
we crave solidarity with you —
in energetic focusing and a life of honest faith.
Amen.

*The soul unto itself is an imperial friend — or the most agonizing spy
an enemy could send.*

　　　　　　　　　　　　　　　　—Emily Dickinson

Biographical Note
_____

A Life of Solitary Creativity   Emily Dickinson (1830–1886) was
one of the greatest American poets of her century, though she published almost
nothing during her lifetime. She wrote while living in seclusion in her home in
Amherst, Massachusetts, with very few connections to others. Her poems
were all short and regular, with mostly slant rhymes. Her most important
topics were her own heart's experiences, though she wrote much about nature
also, especially its significance to the human realm.

7. The Canny Bat Changes Her Name

A clever bat got caught one day
By a cat, and begged: *Friend! EAT NOT ME!*
Alas, said cat, *but birds like you,*
A cat like me cannot set free.

> *No bird am I!* cried bat. *Just look,*
> *I am a mouse from head to toe!*
> Cat looked again, the words were true,
> *Okay,* said cat, *I'll let you go.*

Next day poor bat got caught again,
Another cat! An awful fate!
NO! NO! said bat. *YES! YES!* said cat,
All mice I must exterminate.

> *No mouse am I!* that bat cried out,
> *See, I can fly, I'm like a bird!*
> *Okay,* said cat, *I see your point,*
> And let her go without a word.

So that smart bat gave double thanks
That changing names had pulled her through,
And learned how vital names can be
To cause quick judgments, false or true.

Moral: **A name can make a
world of difference.**

PRAYER to listen for the call of my name

Who am I?
What is my true name?
Holy One, you alone know:
You know when I sit down and when I rise, as the Psalmist says.
You know exactly how many years and days I have left,
what work I may have yet to do,
what human links I am meant to hold together, forge or dissolve,
which of my abilities may be called for next,
what healing role I may have yet to play,
where and when I may lie down at last.
You alone know my life, who I am, my uniqueness.
The value of my life, my inner "self," my *name*,
you alone know.
Will I recognize it when I hear it called?
Will I answer: "Coming"?
May it be so.

Praying Your Story

Do you recall meeting someone with an impossible name? Did it incline you to pre-judge the person somehow? What would be the name God might use for you?

A name can make a world of difference.

PRAYER to Barnabas, a substitute apostle

. . . to listen for my vocation

We thank you, brother Barnabas,
for your liberating work in the early church.
The original Twelve called you into apostleship,
then gave you the new name of Barnabas, "son of encouragement,"
and your advocacy for St. Paul and later for John Mark —
though full of controversy —
opened wide the doors of the church.
Traveling with Paul, when not welcomed at synagogue congregations,
you easily moved into work with gentiles,
and successfully halted any burdensome requirements for converts.
With your companionship now we can in good conscience
also welcome diverse points of view
into the one worldwide community of believers.
Amen.

There was a Levite from the island of Cyprus called Joseph, whom the apostles re-named Barnabas — which means "son of encouragement." He owned a piece of land, and he sold it and brought the money to the apostles.

—Acts 4: 36

Biographical Note

A Life Story of Success and Heartbreak Barnabas was one of the earliest missionaries in the church. He preached in Northern Africa and on his native island of Cyprus, accompanying St. Paul, among others. Their audiences were largely gentiles, and once Greek listeners mistook them to be the gods Zeus and Hermes. Later, he and Paul suffered an irreconcilable disagreement and parted company from then on, surely a heartbreaking conflict for a man of such optimism and faith in others.

8. A Gullible Wolf Is Scared Away

A hungry wolf crept through the woods
      One night as quiet as a mouse,
Until he heard a crying child
      Within a woodsman's tiny house.

Sweet Babe, don't cry! he heard them plead,
You've had what sweets we can provide!
Shhh! Please be still! You'll bring the wolf!
Perhaps a wolf is RIGHT OUTSIDE!

The child grew still, turned white with fear,
And mother blushed to use deceit.
      The wolf, quite sure that he'd been seen,
      Ran off like he had wings for feet.

Moral: **Our fears are often foolish.**

PRAYER not to be compulsively fearful

See, caring God,
we are comically apprehensive!
How our world seems laced with threats!
dread in the morning that the day may be tragic,
dread at night that the darkness may contain unseen evils.
Without courageous, upbeat people around us,
it's a sad, dark, fearsome world.
We need them nearby in our family and community,
deep in our historical memory
and knit to our hearts as we go forward into the unknown.
As you have given courage to heroes we have known,
be as generous with us — give us strength too.
Enlighten our hearts with an alertness for your comforting presence.
With the memory of our saints, personal and historical,
show us that the path ahead is manageable,
that we can have courage as they have had.
Without courage, our days fill up with foolishness.
With it, all things are possible.
Amen.

Praying Your Story

Have you ever feared meeting someone who later became a friend?
Did you ever find a celebrity easy to talk to? Freed from a fearful
bias, what do you think God's view of people might be like?

Our fears are often foolish.

PRAYER to the martyr Blandina, woman slave

. . . not to be fearful

Slave-woman Blandina, we remember your name and your heroism,
when you fearlessly refused to surrender to an unjust Roman law
or commit a public dishonesty.
You confessed to the end your own truth:
that the God of Jesus is a God of justice, non-violence and love,
and that the world must become a circle of friendship
based on the graciousness of the living God.
You are our theologian now as we try to stand in the same circle
and to be like you in witnessing to belief in a God
passionate for justice and truth.
Amen.

The point is not just to include women in existing narrative structures in order to make the dominant paradigm look inclusive; . . . rather, the goal is to reshape that narrative paradigm so that female perspectives are as central as male ones in a community of mutuality.
　　　　　　　　　　　　　　　　　　　—Elizabeth Johnson

Biographical Note

Their Slave and Their Sister Blandina was a slave woman martyred along with forty-seven other people in Lyons around 177 C.E. The woman to whom she was enslaved was also martyred at the same time, and they died together like sisters and equals. Everyone found in Blandina a model of strength who persevered in faith despite the threat of death.

Part II

Love Can Make
Fools of Us

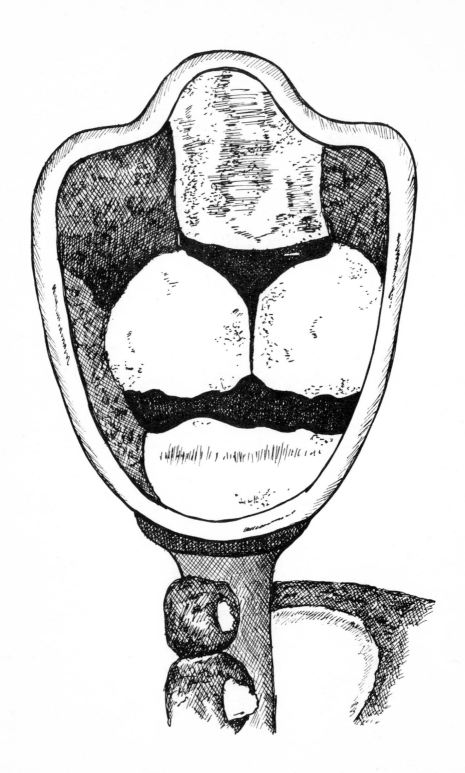

9. An Amorous Lion Becomes a Fool

A fearsome young lion one day fell in love
With a woodcutter's daughter, as sweet as a dove.
      So the lion strode up to their home in the wood,
      And he roared out his passion as loud as he could.

I must marry that maiden! Woodcutter, he said,
But the father's great heart was stricken with dread.
      He was scared to say *No* to the frightening beast,
      Yet he feared a young wife might soon be deceased.

He thought up a trick: With the lion so smitten
Perhaps he could turn the beast into a kitten.
   King Lion, he said, *your great teeth and sharp mitts*
   Have frightened my daughter half out of her wits.
If you pull out your teeth, if you pare down your claws,
I am sure she will be less afraid than she was.

The lion gave in, and came back looking weird
With his claws sanded down and his teeth disappeared,
      May I marry her now? he said (minus the roar).
      BEGONE! laughed the dad, and drove him from the door.

Moral: **Love can make fools
of us.**

PRAYER for foolish lovers

Loving Spirit, reader of hearts,
of course you see how brokenhearted we all are at times:
Some hearts scarred, some crushed, some destroyed.
What agony beyond imagining must be your aching empathy with us!
Philosophers have despaired of speaking of you, much less *to* you,
so beyond comprehension is your own heart —
and how hopeless our words.
Our knowledge of it all is only a cloud and darkness.

Still, the sun rises each day, lovers awake to lovers,
and our deepest self chooses to hope.
We shall send our battered hearts out again,
believing there is for us all, including you, a land beyond heartbreak,
where love alone reigns,
and all wounds are forgotten at last.
May it be so.

Praying Your Story

Do you remember falling in love, your preoccupation with the loved one, what it felt like to accept someone so totally, so non-judgmentally? Isn't that the way God loves you?

Love can make fools of us.

PRAYER to Abbess Heloise, love's heroine

. . . to love generously

We turn to you, heroic Abbess Heloise, to be our teacher
of a love fully human, endlessly promising, but potentially tragic.
We are all caught up in the mystery of human love,
and your refusal to attempt to substitute an unreal "love of God"
for your feelings for your beloved Abelard,
the father of your only child,
is a mark of your admirable integrity.
You gave your life to writing and service to the needy,
but it was always sparked by passion and honesty.
We hope, like you, to reverence all our relationships,
true to their demands to the end.
Amen.

You know, beloved, as the whole world knows, how much I have lost in you.
— Abbess Heloise

Let us be known by the scars of love that mark our faces.
— Rumi

Biographical Note
———————

A Story of Love and Non-Conformity As a brilliant and beautiful young seventeen-year-old, Heloise (1100–1164) was given as a tutor the most famous scholar in France, Abelard, a man in his mid-thirties. They fell in love, and their astonishing love affair — and lifelong separation — makes up one of the most well-known and tragic love stories of all time. Heloise finally became the Abbess of the Convent of the Paraclete in Paris, and there Abelard was buried. Twenty-one years later Heloise died, and was buried beside him.

10. Some Revelers Forget Past Lessons

Some carefree revelers took a ship
To sea so they could eat and drink
Without restraint or any care
For what the gods above might think.

But soon the waves became so high
Their little ship tossed up and down,
And whirlwinds roared above their heads
And they felt sure that they would DROWN.

Dear Gods! they cried, *dear Powers Above,*
Come to our aid lest we all die!
And soon that storm grew calm and still,
And sunbeams glowed throughout the sky.

Pass out the wine! proclaimed the host,
No need to fear these placid skies!
NO, WAIT! Another voice cried out,
It was the steersman, brave and wise.

Enjoy your fun, he softly said,
But like the wise, not like the fool.
Keep death's dark nearness in your mind,
And moderation as your rule.

***Moral:* The thought of death
can make us wise.**

PRAYER to stay in touch with Sister Death

Marvelous God, genius of surprises,
dazzling me daily and hourly with life around me,
the human, the cosmic, the microcosmic.
Yet with particular affection,
you have located me in a special human circle,
and wrapped me in my personal calendar —
until now.
Of course that human circle is temporary,
and that calendar ends somewhere —
which should not be, I pray, the greatest surprise of life.
It's the one thing about the future that's certain.
So let me live each day in gratitude and wisdom,
and be always ready for the expected visit of Sister Death
so I may give her an appropriate welcome.
Amen.

Praying Your Story

Have you been surprised with the news that someone you knew had died? Do you find it hard at times to imagine the deceased as really dead? Do God and death go together for you?

The thought of death can make us wise.

PRAYER to Joseph of Nazareth, parent of Jesus

. . . for a happy death

Holy Joseph, father of Jesus
and husband to his gifted, revolutionary mother,
be our companion spirit today
as you were companion to your son in carpentering.
Accompany us in our service to others,
so we may help repair — to the best of our ability —
the brokenness in human life around us.
May both you and your son be with us in this work
so our energies and skills may be helpful to others
and our presence and caringness
a useful benefit to our life companions.
Amen.

Now when they had departed, behold, an angel of the Lord appeared to Joseph in a dream and said, "Rise, take the child and his mother and flee to Egypt, and remain there till I tell you, for Herod is about to search for the child to destroy him." And he rose and took the child and his mother by night and departed to Egypt and remained there until the death of Herod.

—Matthew 2: 13-16

Biographical Note
_____

Obedient to Grace Little is known of Joseph, the legendary foster-father of Jesus and life companion of Mary. He is identified as a carpenter in the Gospel text itself, and it was traditional that a son would follow in the craft of his father. Surely they worked together in the many calls for carpentering in the geographical area around their home. Since Joseph is not mentioned later in the Gospels and is not present at the time of Jesus' death, it is assumed he had died while Jesus was young, with himself and Mary at his bedside. Thus, Joseph was named saint of a happy death.

11. A Wolf Becomes Proud of Its Shadow

One day at sunset on a hill
A wolf was quite surprised
To see the shadow of himself
Immensely oversized.

> *Good God, it's me! How huge I am!*
> *How frightening! How grim!*
> He broke into an ice cold sweat:
> It even frightened *HIM.*

How big I am! I should be king!
A super-wolf, he cried.
Then he let out a prideful growl
That echoed far and wide.

> It echoed far enough to reach
> A lion with a wish
> To eat an evening pot luck meal
> But lacked a good main dish.

With one great leap he grabbed the wolf,
Who cried out in confusion.
How DUMB I was not to suspect
My power was an illusion.

Moral: **Test your beliefs before**
you act on them.

PRAYER to be humble despite a brilliant career

My Pulitzer Prize is less important
than my unwritten book of letters to you, Holy One,
prayers and memoirs you have read in my heart.
My McArthur Foundation grant was helpful,
but not to my most brilliant achievement: surrender to reality.
The Nobel Peace Award put money in the bank,
but I value more my episodes of compassion, however minimal.
The Congressional Medal of Honor gave me a few proud moments,
but not more proud than the ten-thousand times I swallowed my pride.

When you add it all up (and will you not add it all up?),
it's a brilliant career,
yet nothing to be self-absorbed about.
Make me honest and humble, Holy Sophia,
despite stellar achievements.
Amen.

Praying Your Story

Do you usually think of yourself as immortal, unthreatened by sickness and death? Why is it so hard to make death a part of one's mind-set? Can the thought of God help?

Test your beliefs before you act on them.

PRAYER to Teresa of Avila, prioress and reformer

. . . to trust in inspiration

Much traveled, passionate reformer of the medieval church, Teresa,
holy companion to our lives,
be with us.
We need that Jewish passion in the church again, like yours,
like your friend John of the Cross's —
and like the prophetic Jesus himself.
Rooted as you were in traditional psalms and stories,
with a sure hand you reshaped the Catholic Church.
At your death they quickly canonized you
and named you "Doctor of the Church,"
but the honors failed to have their targeted effect:
to neutralize your reformer's voice.
Be a courageous sister to us all.
When our shyness would make us silent, you are our model of a protestor,
passionate, if not brash.
When we would despair of lifeless traditions,
give us the verve to invent a better future for our religion.
Lead us, uncompromising Mother Teresa,
in the human dance of honesty and good sense.
We want to learn the prudent rhythms of your irrepressible spirit.
Amen.

Prayer is, in my view, nothing but friendly conversation, and frequent
solitary exchanges with someone whom we know loves us.
> —Teresa of Avila

Biographical Note

The Tale of an Irresistible Force Teresa of Avila (1515–1582)
has been named a Doctor of the Church by reason of her writings on spirituality,
but it was her travels and her reformist energies that had the most effect in her
own day. She was the foundress of seventeen convents in Spain and became a
great force for honesty and faith in the church. She experienced great love for
God and concern for others, and her strong inner spirit overcame illness, failure
and disappointment to effect great improvement in the church.

12. A Greedy Lion Loses His Dinner

A ravenous lion found a rabbit asleep
And instantly planned to assail him.
So without even saying a Prayer Before Meals,
He opened his mouth to inhale him.

When, lo, in his sight a fat reindeer ran by,
The first reindeer seen in this venue.
Ah, why have commonplace rabbit, said lion,
I'll try what is new on the menu.

But the deer got away. *Oh, well,* said the lion,
I guess I'll just have bunny chowder.
But when he came back very ready to eat,
The rabbit had taken a POWDER.

Moral: **Desire for more can
undo what you have.**

PRAYER to take setbacks without whining

God of Life and of Death,
you have spun me twirling around the sun so many times,
my mortal heart pumping away a hundred thousand times a day,
my lungs filling and emptying twenty-four thousand times a day,
all my bodily systems functioning involuntarily — but wonderfully —
at nature's command.
One of these days, at nature's command, it will all cease,
and, with the help of family and friends,
I'll return my body to the earth from which it was formed,
heart still at last, lungs airless and collapsed.
Instinctively, I would desire ever more life,
but how foolish it would be to substitute my shortsighted ambitions
for the vision of God.

I have no complaints. I've enjoyed my innings.
Others will live in my house, sleep in my bed: So be it.
For all its colossal disappointments,
life is much like forty years in the desert,
where everybody gets home in the last chapter.
So, whine not, my soul:
Though pursued by death all our days,
we shall outwit it in the end.
What more could we ask?
Amen.

Praying your story

Can you think of some friend whose life has been luckier than yours? Has envy ever made your days less happy? Might God's views on this subject be different than yours?

Desire for more can undo what you have.

PRAYER to Mary of Nazareth, Mother of Jesus

. . . for wisdom and humility

Mystery-shrouded mother of a messianic son,
sister to marginalized women the world over,
through all the veils of myth and Gospel-telling
we perceive you vaguely across 2,000 years,
a village woman, homemaker-wife of a carpenter,
mothering many children, faithful to your parenting role.
With your permission we must take you down from history's pedestal
and into the commonplace communion of saints — where we all are.
We, all your plain sisters and brothers, do ourselves know something
of the bewilderment of your life on earth
leading up to the catastrophe of the cross whereon Jesus died.
At times when our own lives are taking place beneath that cross,
we reverently share your grief as we know you share in ours,
inspired by you to look from the darkness
toward a sunrise of hope.
Like you, may we find the grace
to say *"Fiat," Yes*, to our life just as it unfolds.
Amen.

My soul magnifies my God, and my spirit rejoices in loving help from the God of Mystery.

—Mary of Nazareth, Luke 1: 46-47

Biographical Note

The Life of a Blessed Mother We know remarkably little historically about the mother of Jesus — but we have a virtual avalanche of theological writing about her. The information in the early chapters of Luke's Gospel may well be poetical "theology" built on later perceptions of the role of Jesus in Salvation History. Mary is remembered first as a revolutionary woman, uttering the song of the Magnificat — a declaration of the victory of the oppressed over the ruling class. She is all but left out of the four Gospels until her son's last days, and there she appears, faithful to him to the end. She obviously had an important role in the early church community, and is now known mostly in her symbolic role as Mother of the Church.

13. A Lovesick Cat Becomes a Woman

A lovesick cat once longed to have
Her master as her lover.
So Goddess Venus took her part
And made a woman of her.

She quickly won the master's heart
They were to wed in style!
But as the priest began to speak,
A mouse ran up the aisle!

> The bride let out an awful snarl
> And raced after the mouse
> Until it vanished down a hole
> That was its little house.

> The master screamed: *You chased a mouse!*
> *What horror could be greater!*
> *Don't sweat the small stuff,* she replied,
> *I'll catch real big ones later.*

ENOUGH! said Venus, *You have failed*
To humanize your soul!
So she was made a cat again,
A more befitting role.

Moral: **Radical human change
is rare.**

PRAYER to be the cat I was meant to be

Do you not enjoy, Holy Spirit, the coolness of your creation, the cat?
Its independence? Its mystery? Its serenity?
Hiding a self-defined soul somewhere behind an ambivalent visage.
Never giving away its heart.
Having an infinite capacity to stretch, then to rest.
Guiltless: caring little what anyone is thinking of it.
Isn't that the cat I was meant to be?
Not in a hurry, yet explosively recoiled;
Moving on with life as though all will be well,
And there's ultimately nothing absurd,
Knowing any minute might get interesting and ready to be part of it.
Gracefully.
Affectionately.
Self-contented first,
but alert, ready at all times to leap — or flop.
Make me the cat I was meant to be.
Amen.

Praying Your Story

Can you recall any distinctive childhood, and childish, characteristic that is still part of your makeup, something you never got over? A compassionate, Divine Parent might enjoy that in you.

Radical human change is rare.

PRAYER to Etty Hillesum, Dutch Shoah victim

. . . to invent an authentic self

It is impossible to place you, unique and saintly Etty Hillesum,
in some category of human heroics.
You invented your own spirituality from within,
indentifying that inner feeling of universal love
with your truest self, with the divine.
Woman of passion and of honesty,
you would be uncomfortable not to be in solidarity
with your own Jewish people
as they suffered the murderous onslaught of the Nazi Shoah,
and you voluntarily gave up your safety to be with them.
Your boundless inner strength is a wonder to us,
and makes it possible for us to keep hoping for the ultimate victory of
justice and love despite what evils may come.
Amen.

*I know what may lie in wait for us. . . . And yet I find life beautiful
and meaningful.*

—Etty Hillesum

Biographical Note

The Story of an Interrupted Life Etty Hillesum (1914–1943)
was a young Jewish woman who lived in Holland during the Nazi occupation
and who died as one of the victims of the Holocaust. Her carefully kept diary
— discovered years after her death and now published as *An Interrupted Life*
— recorded the events in her spirituality dedicated to the supreme power of
love, of forgiveness and the meaningfulness of all that is. Never formally
religious, she found the divine within herself and in her embodied experiences
of love and non-violence. She was put to death on November 30 at the age of
twenty-nine.

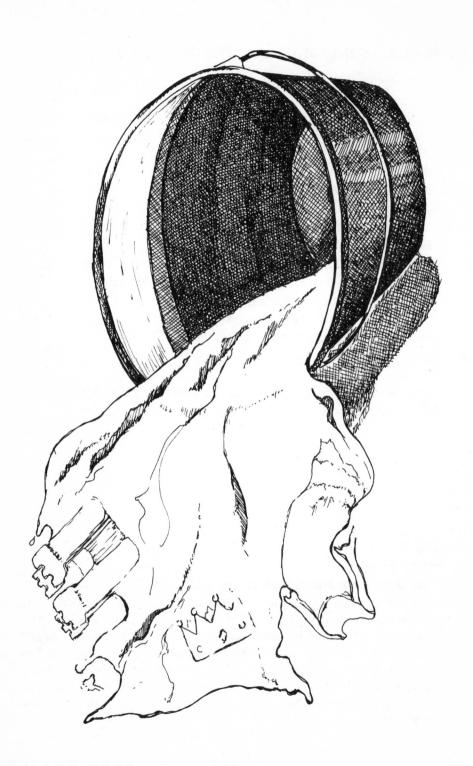

14. A Milkmaid Dreams Too Much

A milkmaid walked along a road
       With a bucket of milk on her head.
Let's see! How many dozen eggs
       Could I buy with this milk? she said.

Ten dozen at least, she thought she'd get,
       So a hundred chicks I'll own,
And half I'll sell and half I'll keep
       And raise them till they're grown.

Then THEY'LL lay eggs on every side,
       Which I'll sell at the marketplace,
And buy me a gown which will charm a prince
       Whom I'll capture without a chase.

He'll bow like this! And I'll bow to him —
       But her bow sent her milk for a spin,
And down came her dreams of a royal throne
       With a castle and prince thrown in.

Moral: **Smart daydreamers
keep one eye open.**

PRAYER not to live in dreamland

Holy Fire at the center of life,
if I travel inward seeking you,
into a human cell and beyond, to the level of atoms,
then further beyond into the nucleus
and deeper into the DNA,
then beneath a single proton there and into the swirling quarks:
Are you there?
You are!
You make it all happen!
You are the inner engine of everything,
even of my own most inner life.
O Sacred Lover, set me aflame with your unimaginable fire.
Awaken me from the dreamland
where what seems to exist is only what I can see visibly,
which makes an absurd dreamland of our human life,
with no loving Source, no purpose, no destiny.
Be to me not just an occasional thought,
but the very pulse of an awakened life.
Amen.

Praying Your Story

Remember your wildest, most unlikely dream of what might happen,
something you once imagined to be your future? "Nothing is too
wonderful to exist," said Faraday. Does God not love dreamers?

Smart daydreamers keep one eye open.

PRAYER to Mother Hagar, second wife to Abraham

. . . to accept reality as it is

If it be true
that "blessed are the poor, blessed are the meek,
blessed are those who mourn,"
then you are a blessed memory, holy mother Hagar,
model for all who live in painful submission, poverty and servitude,
yet remain resilient with vitality and realism.
You kept faith in God through it all.
Driven from your home with your child,
enduring domestic violence and homelessness,
our faithful Creator still led you to water in the desert.
And you became a witness to the God greater than our hearts,
who "makes a way out of no way,"
not a dream god but the greatest Reality:
the ultimate dream come true.
Whatever be our personal plight,
the empowering memory of you will strengthen us through it all.
Amen.

I have seen the one who sees me.
                                        —Hagar, Genesis 16: 13

Biographical Note
_____

Famous in Myth and History   Hagar's story occurs in chapter 16
of the Book of Genesis. She was an Egyptian slave woman who was, in effect,
the second wife of Abraham and who became the mother of Ishmael. Dismissed
from Abraham's home, Hagar and her son wandered in the desert until their
provisions gave out, and they would have died of thirst had not God directed
them to a well. Ishmael became a mighty warrior and the father of twelve
sons. Both are highly honored by Arab peoples.

15. The Greedy Dog Loses His Bone

A greedy dog once found a bone
So big he could hardly carry it.
I'll take this home, he told himself,
And there I'll safely bury it.

But as he leaped a tiny stream
With energy and vigor,
He saw a dog reflected there
Whose bone looked even bigger.

He LUNGED! Alas, he lost his bone
And the river tasted bitter,
His bone was gone, and he went home
A sad but wiser critter.

Moral: **The greedy may lose everything.**

PRAYER to be less greedy

God of Goodness,
those whom humans most admire are the open-handed and generous,
mothers rich in caringness for every loved one in need,
fathers prodigal with all they have,
friends who make our joys and concerns their own.
Give us such prodigal trust in you
that we will not be self-absorbed and grasping.
But also free us from spiritual greediness —
that need to appear virtuously correct and innocent —
depending instead on our forgiveness of others
to be shriven of our own shortcomings.
Teach that illusive lesson to my deepest soul
for I always find it hard to believe the Gospel.
Help thou my unbelief.
Amen.

Praying Your Story

Have you ever been tempted by the gamble: double or nothing?
Were you ever able to quit while winning? When in your life have
you been greedy? Does God blame you?

The greedy may lose everything.

PRAYER to Dorothy Day, champion of the poor

. . . to open our hearts to the poor

Dear reluctant prophetess, Dorothy Day,
your unique life inspires us, your more conventional sisters and brothers.
Your life of solidarity with the poor
unfolded by surprise and happenstance:
It was your bohemian "natural happiness"
       that triggered a conventional faith-life within you;
it was the chance encounter with Peter Maurin
       that focused your own sense of destiny;
it was starting a newspaper
       that later necessitated the centers for feeding and hospitality.
So give us compassion and trust first, generosity later.
In solidarity with you we shall hope that our own lives —
through chance or providence —
will grow in meaning and effectiveness.
Like you, we will take one trustful step after another.
God be our guide.
Amen.

Where were the saints to try to change the social order?
                —Dorothy Day

Biographical Note
_____

A Heart for the Very Poorest Dorothy Day (1897–1980) was founder of the Catholic Worker Movement, which even today supports hundreds of houses of hospitality, feeding and clothing the needy in many American cities. Dorothy Day was an anarchist and, with the assistance of philosopher Peter Maurin, became a religious radical, living out literally the Gospel teaching. She was a prodigious author, editor and lecturer, and is an inspiration to thousands to this day.

16. The Prideful Mice Are Defeated

When mice waged war against the cats,
Their casualties were large.
What we need is some leadership,
They said: *Who'll be in charge?*

Four mice held up their paws so they
Got roles quite honorary.
And give us helmets with big horns,
They said, *To prove we're scary.*

Their next war effort failed again
But all the mice stayed whole —
Except the chiefs whose awesome horns
Would not fit down their hole.

Alas, their lives just blew away
As quick as summer breezes,
Like all those who don't want to lead
But just to be BIG CHEESES.

Moral: **High honors can be a
curse.**

PRAYER to be preserved from triumphalism

Compared to your many gifts to me, Holy One,
my earned honors are few, my deserved reproofs many.
At times I can walk in vanity and isolation
as if dressed in honorary robe, hood and stole,
my name adorned with credentials, my mien seriously dignified.
Give me instead the honest pride
of the ant, the butterfly or the city pigeon:
to do my work, celebrate simple joys,
and hold no airs.
I prefer to be an unremarkable member of an astonishing human race
than the laughingstock of heaven.
Amen.

Praying Your Story

What is the most undeserved honor or prize you have ever received?
Did any person ever praise you too highly, making you suspicious?
Does God want you free of peer pressure?

High honors can be a curse.

PRAYER to Dag Hammarskjöld, saintly U.N. leader

. . . for an accurate self-image

We think of you as a kind of martyr,
man of mystery, Dag Hammarskjöld, first leader of the United Nations,
top man of honor in the world, modest in your own eyes:
the plane crash may well have been a plot against your peace mission.
Still, you had surrendered your life long before that,
in total dedication to the needs of the world.
This we discovered in your one — but posthumous — publication,
the secret "Markings" in your journal,
recording where and when you found meaning, and what you believed,
enriching us all with a classic documentation of a private spirituality.
"Not I, but God in me," you wrote the day of your election.
That is a rich and dangerous motto for humankind
for it can be a fountain of courage.
We thank you for your quiet holiness
and self-effacing modesty,
mysterious brother in the communion of saints.
Amen.

Not I, but God in me.

—Dag Hammerskjöld

Biographical Note

A Story of Surreptitious Saintliness Dag Hammerskjöld (1905–1961), a former banker and deputy foreign minister of Sweden, served as Secretary General of the U.N. from 1953 until his death in a plane crash in Africa at the age of fifty-six. After his death he was awarded the 1961 Nobel Peace Prize for his efforts to bring peace to the Congo and throughout the world. In 1964 his book of prayers and reflections, *Markings*, was published and became an instant spiritual classic.

Part III

God Helps Those Who Help Themselves

17. A Drowning Priest Learns To Pray

One day a schooner filled with men —
Some young, some old, and one a priest —
Sank in a storm, and all aboard
Felt sure they soon would be deceased!

> The young swam well and helped the old,
> Who nobly their best effort gave,
> But the poor priest just cried and prayed
> Athena-God his life would save.
>
> *A hundred ducats will I pledge!*
> He shouted, *I'm your devotee!*
> *Two hundred! Three! Or even more!*
> *Just come out here and RESCUE ME!*

Just then a sailor swimming near
Cried: *Pray your best, that's not a sin!*
But also move your bloomin' arms!
And that suggestion saved his skin.

Moral: **God helps those who
help themselves.**

PRAYER to grow in awe of God

It's amazing, Awesome Spirit-Force,
how abstracted we can be about what's going on around us.
When we turn to you in prayer,
we assume your attention is centered on human life and death.
Meanwhile, all unseen, for each single human life,
there are 200 million insect lives
that move about us, on us and sometimes in us,
all demanding your divine attention.
Awesome: six billion humans times 200 million bugs.
And what's going on with them?
Male hercules beetles are smashing frontal horns
over females.
Bombardier beetles are defending themselves
by exploding scalding hot propellants (at 100 degrees centigrade)
at their attackers.
Lady bugs, eating aphids in the garden left and right,
are calmly exuding a repulsive fluid
that conveniently drives away their enemies.
It is a massive dramatic scene everywhere on earth,
all of concern to you, Holy Creator and Sustainer.
Hear our prayer?
Yes, but more to the point: Hear our awe!
Amen.

Praying Your Story

Do you remember ever praying for something impossible? Does life sometimes feel too undramatic? What would be the most important thing to pray for?

God Helps Those Who Help Themselves.

PRAYER to Paul of Tarsus, author of the Epistles

. . . to pray always

Leave it to you, Paul of Tarsus, eloquent New Testament author,
to lay on all Christians the impossible task of praying always.
You never did things by half measures.
Originally you visited synagogues,
facilitating not dialogue but the stoning of deviancy,
then, once you had joined the deviants (the Christians),
you traveled the world making converts
and urging them to live and die for Christ —
as you yourself did.
Model of enthusiasm,
totalist in your commitment to Christ,
you prayed to him "always" and urged the same on your followers.
With you, we shall strive to fill our days with prayer,
and our hearts with commitment to the ultimate reign of God.
Amen.

I live, now not I but Christ lives in me.
—Saint Paul, Galatians 2: 20

Biographical Note

─────────

The Story of a Heart on Fire Paul (originally Saul) never met Jesus
of Nazareth during his life and even joined in attacks on his early followers. But
with his mystical experience on the road to Damascus (described in Acts), he
became the greatest evangelizer in favor of the Christian faith. His writings are
works of genius and carry unparalleled weight in the churches to this day. In
contrast to the communities of Matthew, Mark and Luke, Paul joins the Fourth
Evangelist in stressing faith in the very divinity of Jesus, thus severing
Christianity's natural continuity with Judaism and marking it forever as a belief
system that claims superiority over all other religions.

18. A Wise Bear Advises a Traveler

Two traveling friends met a bear one day
In a woods that was much overgrown.
One raced up a tree and left his poor friend
To face the wild creature alone.

   The other had heard that bears never will
   Take a bite of a man that's dead,
   So he lay down flat, and the bear walked up
   And sniffed him from toe to head.

Away went the bear, and down came the friend:
Did that bear speak into your ear?
He anxiously asked. *Tell me what he said!*
It's something I'm eager to hear!

   Said the smiling friend, *He whispered to me*
   A secret surprising but clear,
   Never travel with so-called friends, said that bear,
   Who when needed will just DISAPPEAR.

Moral: **A friend in need is a
friend indeed.**

PRAYER to make my enemies ever more exasperated

Holy God, many fellow travelers on life's pathway
are not, to be honest, really very helpful to our common good.
Many are dedicated to a life simply pursuing domination:
They are really friends to no one.
God bless with a wake-up call those lost in isolation and privilege:
I stand against their politics.
God heal those who exploit the trapped:
Be merciful to them, Holy Spirit, open their eyes.
For my part I know I must throw in my lot with the vulnerable,
with the marginalized, with the crushed and misunderstood.
I long to share my ample freedom with the trapped and the insecure.
I'd like to be worthy of marching under their flag,
wearing their colors, voting on their side.
Nothing more exasperates my enemies: good!
Give me the courage to bug them all my life,
Amen.

Praying Your Story

What is the greatest favor anyone has ever done for you? Have you
ever been able to make a big difference by helping someone? Have
you ever felt inspired by God to assist in some cause?

A friend in need is a friend indeed.

PRAYER to Mother Jones, labor organizer and activist

. . . to speak truth fearlessly to power

Great seraph of justice, plain-speaking Mother Jones,
it was only about 100 years ago that you brought the child-miners up
from underground and fought for workers' rights everywhere, crying:
"Pray for the dead, but fight like hell for the living!"
Unafraid saint of the working have-nots,
stand by us in our efforts to make the Gospel of Justice something real,
with real effects on conscience and on wages.
We find your enthusiasm inspiring,
and dedicate ourselves to labor beside you
on the side of the trapped and vulnerable.
Amen.

Pray for the dead, but fight like hell for the living!
—Mother Jones

Biographical Note

A Champion of Social Justice Mary Harris Jones (1830–1930) was a famous personality in the U.S. labor movement, a union organizer and prophetic voice, helping form local labor unions among coal miners and others. Her own four children, along with her husband, died of yellow fever in Memphis, and thereafter she went into business and finally into the labor movement. She had great influence in raising the wages of workers and in outlawing child labor.

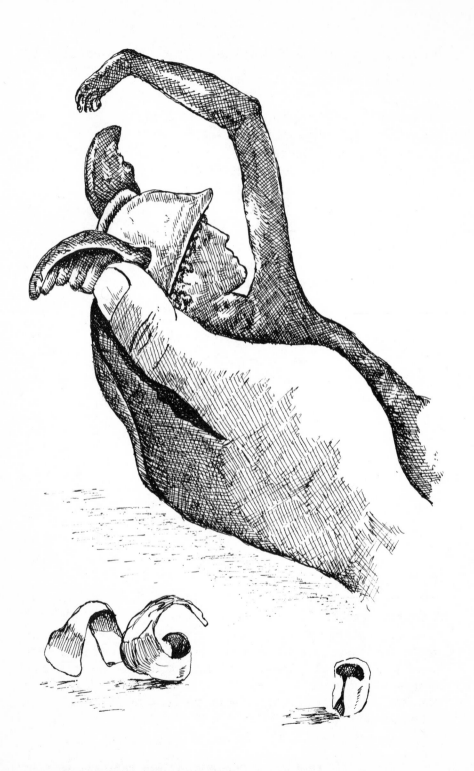

19. A Man Tries To Sell a God

One day a clever craftsman carved
A god and brought him to the mall.
Hermes it was, a work of art,
But no one seemed to care at all.

> Upset, the man stood on a box
> And shouted loud to make his pitch,
> *Wise Friends! This god is full of power,*
> *A power that can make you rich!*

Hold on! remarked a passer-by
Why sell him if he answers prayer?
Use him yourself if that god be
As powerful as you declare!

> He answered: *He has power, of course,*
> *Or Holy Hermes he'd not be!*
> And then his voice dropped to a hush:
> *He's just a bit too SLOW for me.*

***Moral:* Humans prefer gods of
their own making.**

PRAYER forgiving God for slowness in helping

What kind of God are you, mysterious unimaginable Spirit,
creator of us all?
You are not quick to come to the aid of those who cry to you.
You have apparently chosen not to be omnipotent,
to have no power to save those you love from even terrible pain.
How can this be?
Yet forgive you we must: Your choice has to be best.
You are decidedly a Strange Spirit, an Enigmatic Entity.
Is "God" the best name for you?
You do not occupy space like a cloud;
you do not move about like the air.
Some wouldn't even call you a "being."
You are profoundly unlike us who think discursively,
who love conditionally,
who exist contingently.
We name you Father, Mother — the most noble metaphors we know:
Sister, Brother, Ocean, Sky — all our fondest images . . .
yet while somewhat like these, you are far more their unlike.
You escape our minds, Holy One —
but, look, not our hearts . . .
which hunger still to rest in you.
Amen.

Praying Your Story

Do you remember the God of your childhood? Of your school days?
Is not the mystery of God more and more elusive as life goes on?
Do you ever find God beyond words?

Humans prefer gods of their own making.

PRAYER to Simone Weil, modern interfaith saint

. . . to remain faithful to faith

Brilliant, heroic Simone Weil, your life path mystifies us.
We deeply admire your instinctive compassion
for all the marginalized of the earth,
yet wonder what part of it we can relate to.
You remained all your life unbaptized and outside any faith community,
yet felt united to Christ and one with his Gospel.
Who was your God?
While we assume your calling was unique to you,
still, we ultimately think of you as a trustworthy guide
to both spirituality and social attitudes,
valuing above all as you did a solidarity with the most deprived,
and "the immense and unfortunate multitude of unbelievers."
Be a sister to us, Simone,
and a helpful companion in both our inner and public life.
Amen.

Today it is not nearly enough merely to be a saint; but we must have the saintliness demanded by the present moment, a new saintliness.

—Simone Weil

Biographical Note

The Life of a Mystical Outsider Simone Weil (1909–1943) was a philosopher and teacher in France during the Spanish Civil War and, in her compassion for the oppressed, went to Spain to assist the unsuccessful rebellion. Her books demonstrate a unique spirituality based solidly on the Christian Gospels, though she remained outside the institutional church all her life. She had a rare inner drive to share in the experience of the working class, and put herself at the service of forces aimed at bettering their lot.

20. The Clever Donkey Tricks a Wolf

A donkey sensed a hungry wolf
Was slithering about,
So he began to limp and moan
Until the wolf cried out:
> *What makes you limp, my donkey friend?*
> *Why such a mournful bray?*

> *Oh, wolf, this thorn stuck in my hoof*
> *Has cut my foot all day.*
> > *And it would cut your tender mouth*
> > *If you devoured me,*
> > *So pull this thorn before you bite!*
> > *Avoid that agony!*

So wolf picked up that donkey's hoof
And looked up underneath,
And WHAM! the donkey kicked just once
And wolf lost all his teeth.

Ah, what a fool I was, lisped wolf,
As donkey turned to flee,
To trust the words of anyone
Who lives in fear of me.

Moral: **No one relates honestly**
to those they fear.

PRAYER against fear

Holy One,
in no way do I really fear you,
yet I am full of anxiety, I know not why;
but you know.
Is it because I have felt pain too often:
pain of disappointment, of failure, of humiliation,
of misunderstanding, of bodily limitation and mortality?
Or is it just my fear of the dark, of the unknown, of insecurity?
Still, I know you have given us cures for fear:
by opening our hearts to others,
overcoming the delusion that we must be alone
or the hallucination that we are hopelessly unlovable.
God of love, be near.
Amen.

Praying Your Story

When have you had to relate to someone you feared? Do you avoid problematic people, those who give you unpleasant feelings? Is God ever fearful?

No one relates honestly to those they fear.

PRAYER to Steven Biko, South African hero

. . . for courage to fight confidently

Holy Steven Biko, martyr and saint
for hundreds of thousands of black South Africans,
you gave them the simple key to political power when you advised:
"Begin to look at yourself as a human being!"
You model for us the courage to enlighten our cruel society
even if in a small way.
Though you died under torture in 1977,
your spirit inspires us to boldly claim — whatever the cost —
that we are no less than human beings,
not just economic units,
not just votes,
not just workers or numbers or problems,
but full human beings,
siblings to all the humans on the earth,
co-creators of human life as it is,
companions to all who have lived, forebears of all who will be,
children of the only God.
Woe to those who would mistreat us.
Amen.

Begin to look at yourself as a human being!
—Steven Biko

Biographical Note
———————

A Martyr for Our Time   Steven Biko (1946–1977), a South African
political leader, died in police custody on September 12, 1977, at the age of
thirty. It was Biko who had inherited the leadership of black South Africa after
the jailing of Nelson Mandela, and he became founder of the Black Consciousness
Movement — which eventually rallied the people of color to oppose and finally
overthrow the white dominated government and the infamous system of apartheid
that kept the races in South Africa separated. He is honored as a hero in the
struggle that achieved black liberation.

21. The Boastful Rooster Loses His Life

Once there was a handsome rooster
      Big of muscle, tall and strong.
Proud he was to frighten every
      Other cock that came along.

One fine day a junior rooster
      Cock-a-doodled in the yard!
Flash! The senior's claws attacked
      And ran off junior, bruised and scarred.

How he strutted then with victory,
      While the hens all clapped and laughed!
Up he flew atop the henhouse,
      Bellowing like he was daft.

But just then a passing eagle
      Heard the noise and swooped right down
And carried off that bragging rooster
      As a lunch for eagle town.

Down below, the junior rooster
      Staggered forth and took a bow,
While all the hens and chicks were clucking
      How *their HERO!* he was now.

Moral: **Only fools praise
themselves.**

PRAYER not to be a buffoon

Ninny I can be, my God, shy to risk embarrassment.
Dunce I can be as well, slow to catch on to the obvious.
Above all do I qualify as clown,
part of the entertainment in this circus world,
patches from head to toe,
tipsily egocentric
and all unconscious of my incongruities.
But let me never be the buffoon,
so set in my convictions that I cannot learn,
a merely saddening sight.
The spiritual path is full of surprises,
but none that will make a tragedy out of me
if I have the grace to keep an open mind
and to take myself lightly.
May it be so.

Praying Your Story

Have you ever felt seriously humiliated? Or conversely, have you ever accidentally won undeserved acclaim? Is honest humility an ideal for you?

Only fools praise themselves.

PRAYER to Patrick, saint of Ireland

. . . to take one's self lightly

Dear holy Patrick, sweetly within reach of our prayer,
wherever you may be,
help us live hale, hardy and joyous as you did,
modest, serviceable and without egotistical ambitions.
Sing for us all with your famous lyrical eloquence,
your stentorian voice and mystical passion,
so we may honor with you the incomprehensible Mystery of Being,
our God.
May that divine brightness,
that unapproachable light,
be reflected in the enlightenment of our consciousness,
and in the lightness of our hearts, rich in knowledge,
in forgiveness of all
and in whimsical irreverence for ourselves.
Perhaps your greatest gift was your cheerful exoneration of the people
who had enslaved you as a youth,
returning after your escape to serve them freely.
Be with us as we all journey with you toward the astonishing unknown.
Amen.

Christ be with me, Christ before me, Christ behind me . . . . Christ in the heart of everyone who thinks of me.
> —Breastplate of St. Patrick

Biographical Note

A Legend Come True Patrick (389–461) initially was kidnapped from Briton by Irish raiders, then escaped — but later returned, believing he had survived the ordeal for the purpose of spreading the Gospel in Ireland. For thirty years he was a wandering bishop there, and the stories of his exploits have become legendary. Irish and non-Irish alike celebrate his memory all over the world.

22. The Grasshoppers Fail To Save for the Future

All summer long the ants had worked
To fill their homes with bread,
So in the winter they could eat
When all the plants were dead.

But grasshoppers with violins
Played music on the lawn
Through summer nights and danced as though
Tomorrow'd never dawn.

And when it snowed, the ants just ate
The bread they had in store,
While grasshoppers with violins
Came hungry to their door.

How DUMB we were, the hoppers cried,
To not plan for tomorrow.
We'd have the life the ants enjoy
And not this world of sorrow.

Moral: **Each day's first task is
to plan for tomorrow.**

PRAYER to become slightly more prodigal

God of the future,
we need patience in being your worshipers:
Your ways are not our ways.
You are prodigal,
pouring out existence and life in every forest and ocean and planet
and across time's unthinkable ages.
Such prodigality, it seems, does not work for mere creatures.
Not being divine, we must be provident instead —
but we may carry it to extremes,
hoarding time and money as if the future were entirely in our hands.
We surrender:
teach us your ways.
A little.
Amen.

Praying Your Story

Recall something you planned, complex and difficult, which came off exactly right. Then think of some wonderful coincidence that happened as if planned by someone. Was it God?

Each day's first task is to plan for tomorrow.

PRAYER to Harriet Tubman, heroic slave woman

. . . to live for others

Are you there, Sister Harriet —
small of stature, towering of heart, pan-cosmic of soul —
now to care about the liberation of us all,
provident in your caringness for those less empowered than yourself,
prodigal with your energies in the service of justice?
We call your name,
believing it is your glory to be remembered,
as you remembered during your life those still enslaved.
We long for untrammeled hearts,
unshackled imaginations
and free-spirited devotion to people in need.
It's a joy to name you, Sister Harriet,
as our guide and companion in every effort we make
to find our own way to freedom each day.
Amen.

I was **free,** *and they should be free.*

—Harriet Tubman

Biographical Note

A Conductor on the Underground Railroad Harriet Tubman (1820?–1913) was a diminutive African slave woman in the U.S. who made nineteen trips back and forth from south to north leading others to freedom. Threats of punishment and all the dangers of cross-country traveling could not dissuade her from her mission. She believed she was companioned by God and all the spirits of heaven. She lived into her nineties, and a book about her published in 1869 made her famous in her own day.

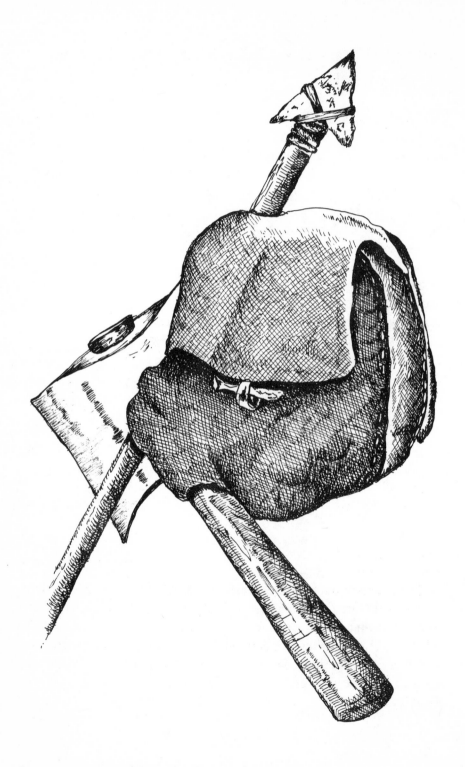

23. The Hunter Hunts Only Tracks

A hunter, fearsome to behold,
One day strapped on his heavy pack,
Took up a long spear in his hands
And slung a big axe on his back.
> Then strode with grit into the woods,
> All camouflaged from head to toe,
> His food pack bristling at his waist
> With skins of wine tied on below.

Have you seen tracks? he asked a man
He found asleep beneath a tree,
Of lions, bears, wild boar and wolves,
Whatever vicious beasts there be?

> The man said, *Oh, I know a place*
> *A lion hides to stalk its prey!*
> *OH, NO!* the hunter quickly said,
> *Just tracks is what I seek today.*

Since it was noon, he sat him down
And drank his wine and ate his bun.
Ah, hunting is a daunting sport,
He said, and slept till day was done.

Moral: Fools prefer appearance to reality.

PRAYER to be daily more droll in my own eyes

God of impenetrable purposes,
I am puzzled by the ridiculous illusions that creep up on me,
whispering of virtue, heroism, immortality.
My eyes are full of quick judgments of others,
while I catch myself posing as a saint, holier than even Thou.
If I am alert, no doubt I shall be daily more droll in my own eyes.
It's humorous: While I am trying to get my head together,
my body is falling apart.
I think perhaps I can make a comeback,
but I really haven't been anywhere.
I smile and say all is not lost,
but, then, where is it?
Do you smile, sprightly Liveliness that energizes the universe?
Did you not invent all the humor in life?
I'll trust you to somehow be in charge of it all.
I'll be going out on a limb if I do,
but other options are even more scary.
Amen.

Praying Your Story

Do you exaggerate? How do you feel when people give you credit
you don't deserve? Are there positive impressions of yourself which
you would like to correct? Does God love only your honest self?

Fools prefer appearance to reality.

PRAYER to Thomas More, lord chancellor of England and martyr

. . . for a lightsome heart

Your integrity, beloved Thomas More,
joined to your wit and intelligence,
makes yours a spirit we shall never forget.
As — even unto death — you would not compromise your convictions,
you inspire us to stand firmly in ours —
though they may be unpopular or subject to ridicule.
You teach us to love the Good News of the Gospel,
to care for the neediest first,
and reverence people diverse in gender, faith and talent.
You had no pretentions, or need to impress;
you stood in your candid reality.
We thank you for your example
that strengthens us in honesty and light-heartedness,
to be, like you, Sir Thomas,
servants of all — "but God's first."
Amen.

Little as I meddle in the conscience of others, I am certain that my conscience belongs to me alone. It is the last thing that a man can do for his salvation, to be at one with himself.

—Thomas More

Biographical Note

A Man for All Seasons Sir Thomas More (1477–1535) was a great English author, statesman and scholar. He served for many years as lord chancellor, the highest judicial official in England, but resigned because he opposed the king's plan to divorce his queen. He was beheaded for refusing to accept the king as head of the English church and thus empowered to alter church law.

24. A Swan Sings To Save Her Life

A wealthy man once kept a goose
And swan together at his house,
The goose to be a feast some day,
The swan to sing songs for his spouse.

> One moonless night he sent the cook
> To catch the goose and dinner make,
> But in the dark the cook misjudged,
> And brought the swan in by mistake.

That swan soon realized her fate
And let her broken heart be known.
Good-bye, sweet earth! Good-bye, sweet friends!
She sang: one long despairing tone.

> *STOP!* cried the cook, *My heart is broke!*
> *This poor swan's song my soul doth wring!*
> *I'll get that other bird for food,*
> *And let this swan live on to sing!*

So swan lived on for years and years,
Enjoying tasty meals and snacks,
And sang her sad and lovely song —
Whenever they brought out the ax.

Moral: **Let your feelings be
known: It may save you.**

PRAYER to tell the honest truth even to God

Holy Mysterious! Creator God!
I'm confused.
Are you the one responsible for all creation?
Or should the credit — or blame — go to intermediaries of some kind:
angelic spirit-inventors who, like ourselves, create in freedom
and are capable of bungling?
Honestly, O God, it seems this option could be true!
Alzheimer's Disease seems a cruel accident.
Nature around us red in tooth and claw
seems a bad system for the web of life.
Hurricanes seem to do far more harm than good.
Birth defects in our beloved children seem so accidental, so preventable —
if one is God.
No, I must not apologize for the doubts:
they are ultimately an enlightening grace.
Behold our hearts: See how we look for love and for loving,
for knowledge and synthesis,
fascinated by the color of the morning sky,
the taste of corn, the joy of skin on skin,
the pleasures of community.
We don't like to complain, but why the gratuitous pain?
We are driven to look to you for meaning — for your presence — in it all.
Be there!
Amen.

Praying Your Story

Do you have some feelings you keep absolutely secret? Have you learned somehow to be ashamed of parts of your inner self? Bring these feelings into God's light.

Let your feelings be known:
It may save you.

PRAYER to Thomas, an apostle of Jesus

. . . to be faithful to doubts

Brother Thomas, biblical champion of doubters,
we admire your style: honoring your feelings
though it set you at odds with others.
Like you, some of us are the searchers, the explorers,
with hearts never at rest while mystery remains.
Today you are enjoying that certainty that eluded you
most of your human life,
and we ask you to be our companion
on our own uncertain earthly journey.
So much deception and credulity
has clouded the path of religious faith over the years
that a skeptical spirit is often the mark of enlightenment now,
and the key to pursuing life's more awesome and disconcerting mysteries.
We long to believe like everyone else.
Help thou our unbelief.
Amen.

Unless I see the holes that the nails made in his hands and feet, and put my finger into the holes they made, and unless I can put my hand into his side, I refuse to believe.

—Thomas the Apostle, John 20: 25

Biographical Note
_____

A Man of Firm Doubts and Firm Convictions Thomas is named among the first disciples of Jesus in all four Gospel accounts. But in John he is given a much more distinct character, doubting early on Jesus' likelihood of success, denying he understood "the Way" Jesus often spoke about, and after Jesus' execution refusing to believe the apostles had experienced a visit from him risen out of death and now alive. He supposedly evangelized India, and in the sixteenth century Portuguese explorers in southern India found a Christian community calling themselves "St. Thomas Christians."

Part IV

We Often Are
Our Own Worst Enemies

25. An Eagle Dies a Bitter Death

An eagle dives from a mountaintop,
Then over tall green trees it swings,
    Exalting in the naked power
      Of feathers plied by eagle's wings.

Too late she sees an arrow flash!
It strikes her heart! She feels the sting!
With grief she sees the arrow's guides
Are feathers dropped from her own wing!

What DOUBLE pain, the eagle cries!
It's bad enough to wounded be,
But even worse, to think the dart
Was helped by guides supplied by me.

Moral: **We are often our own**
worst enemy.

PRAYER not to die unexpectedly

Can I befriend death somehow, seeing your arms welcoming me?
Shall you, Holy Darkness, someday emerge from the cloud of unknowing
in which you hide?
Shall we have our day together at last, Creator of All?
For a long day I have been hunting for signs of you
here in the forest of appearance and illusion,
through the thickets of distractibility,
across the swamps of bewilderment.
Finding you, awesome Quarry, will be a moment of relief:
I'll rejoice to tell myself I need carry the burden of doubt no more.
And will I then have my own public day of fame: a funeral?
All those people concentrating on me? How embarrassing!
But gratifying too, for my counselors will be proved right.
I *am* worthy of unconditional love — for an hour.
And then the city will move on.
On earth I'll be just yesterday's obit.
But in the land of promise, I'll be the new arrival.
So be it.

Praying Your Story

Can you imagine your own death? Where might you be? Who might
be there? What would you like your final words to be? Have you
brought this to God?

We are often our own worst enemy.

PRAYER to Thomas Becket, martyred archbishop

. . . to befriend Sister Death

Holy man Thomas Becket,
as you were being murderously assaulted for your integrity and honesty,
you shouted, "Into thy hands I commend my spirit,"
a death prayer from the lips of the proto-martyr Jesus of Nazareth,
and a model for our own.
You had to live many years with the expectation of death,
but did so with grace.
In truth, your honesty did you in:
Killed by order of your beloved friend, the king,
you played your life's role courageously to its bitter end.
May we do the same, brother Thomas, in communion with you.
Amen.

Your swords are less ready to strike than is my spirit for martyrdom.
—Thomas Becket

Biographical Note

A Story of Murder in the Cathedral Thomas Becket (1118–1170) was the Catholic archbishop of Canterbury who became serious about his spirituality when appointed chancellor of England. In bitter conflicts with the king — at one time his intimate friend — he was murdered in his cathedral by knights as a favor to the king. He is now honored in England as a saint with a shrine at Canterbury in his memory, his name famous for honesty and courage.

26. The Foolish Crab Moves to the Land

A crab once climbed out of the sea
To take a walk on land.
Oh, this is where I ought to live,
He said, *The breeze is simply grand!*

Just then a starving fox ran by
And saw that wandering fool.
Ah-ha! Crab legs for lunch, he thought,
And he began to drool.

One jump and crab was in his teeth!
Cried crab, *I'm such a DOPE!*
I lost the pleasant life I had
To chase a phantom hope.

Moral: **It is wise to appreciate what you have.**

PRAYER to want what you have

Mystery of love and darkness,
I would feel satisfied today
if I could just find adequate words for this demanding prayer,
but it's hard.
Words fail because what I must ask is essentially absurd.
How can I be satisfied with a warm rising sun
while there are clouds somewhere bristling with tornadoes?
How can I satisfactorily rejoice in my child's face
knowing the clock is ticking toward tears and diminishment?
How can the gift of sexuality be satisfactory
when in the long run it produces anguish as well as ecstasy,
death as well as life?
How can I enjoy satisfaction
when every phone book lists prisons, cancer clinics,
shelters for battered women and food shelves for the homeless,
all not far from me?
What troubling resources for a community to have!
Yet we are advised to want what we have!
Have you a reply?
I'll imagine you do. That has to be enough.
Amen.

Praying Your Story

Do you have friends whose hearts astonish you in their ability to cope with hardship? What do you make of poor people who get by with very little? What is in God's heart for them?

It is wise to appreciate what you have.

PRAYER to George Herbert, English priest and poet

. . . to learn to defer gratification wisely

Brilliant, devout George Herbert,
you gave up public success to become a man for others,
yet lived only three short years in ministry.
We knew you on earth as loving husband, ritual servant and man of piety,
but your truer calling,
which you — and the Divine Mystery — kept hidden until your death,
was poetry.
Companion us as you did your own little flock
to live contentedly where life has placed us,
accepting the prose of our daily work
and, when necessary, deferring its poetry.
May we bring imagination to our work,
and service to our creativity,
with anguish in our solidarity with the human race,
but an underground river of contentment
in our surrender to a larger providence.
Perhaps we too shall discover truer blossoming after death
with the full effect of our work deferred
until affirmed in the land of hope.
Amen.

Prayer . . . is the soul in paraphrase, the heart in pilgrimage, the Christian plummet sounding heaven and earth.
                                        —George Herbert

Biographical Note
_____

Publicly Priest, Privately Poet   George Herbert (1593–1633), ordained a priest in 1626, was a leading English poet of Elizabethan England. His collected poems were not published until his death, but then made his name famous. His simple plain verse had a unique quality of clarity and wit, and his writing testifies to his deep faith and commitment to God.

27. A Reckless Deer Takes One Bite Too Many

A deer as swift as any wind
Met hunters armed and well-equipped.
So off it ran into the woods
And under hanging vines it slipped.

    The hunters passed right by the vine
    Not noticing the deer beneath,
    And deer stayed still — until she smelled
    Delicious greens right near her teeth.

Without a thought she took a bite!
Returning hunters caught her slip!
As fatal arrows struck her heart
She cried: *How COSTLY was that nip!*

Moral: **Success makes fools
incautious.**

PRAYER not to indulge unreasonable desires

Hear our prayer, Holy Spirit,
not to drift into dreams of the impossible:
for final justice in the human world,
for full environmental health for our earthly home,
for the ending of human tears
and the ecstasy of full human creativity everywhere.
Let us take instead one firm step forward
in reaching out to help rescue the earth's resources,
light one candle against the darkness of hatred,
or relay one smile to a fellow sojourner along life's road.
We know by now that nothing can be perfect in this life,
but our incautious hearts beat on,
reaching for perfection
for reasons both instinctive and ambivalent.
Amen.

Praying Your Story

What was the silliest hope you've ever had? Are there still some unreal hopes in your heart? Are you cautious enough in planning for the future? Does God urge you to take risks?

Success makes fools incautious.

PRAYER to Mary Magdalene, beloved friend of Jesus

. . . to bide our time

Forgotten church-founder, Mary Magdelene,
cured of seven demons and crucial in Gospel history,
many of us feel the weight of demons of our own: Be our companion.
Your holy role in history was not only to model total discipleship
by remaining with Jesus throughout the hours of his terrible death,
but, since you were among the very first
to be blessed by a vision of the risen Messiah,
it was you who was chosen to first announce that good news to the apostles —
before they then brought it to the world.
The second century knew you as "apostle to the apostles."
Quickly thereafter your memory disappeared,
erasing from the record
the presence of so many women among Jesus' intimate disciples,
and conceding church leadership exclusively to men,
a misdirection we all endure even to our own time.
You are the model, Mary, of sovereign self-possession
despite the temptation to indulge in short-term victories
against the cultural windstorm of prejudice against your gender.
You could bide your time.
Centuries pass, but now at last women's voices are heard.
Mary! We call your name as Jesus did.
Be with us in witnessing the best of news to the world: Jesus lives.
Amen.

I have seen the Lord!
                                        —Mary Magdelene, to the apostles in hiding

Biographical Note

The Greatest Story Never Told Mary *Magdelene* was called by
that name because she was born in the village of Magdala, but Jesus called her
simply "Mary." Luke gives her name at the head of a list of women of Galilee
(Luke 8: 2). She is sometimes confused with "the woman who was a sinner" in
this same Gospel, but that had to be another person altogether. Mary Magdelene
is now honored in her own right, especially as a heroine to other women who
are similarly forgotten and demeaned in the patriarchal church.

28. The Foolhardy Shepherd Rears Wolf Cubs

O, look how CUTE! a shepherd said
When he found wolf cubs fast asleep.
I'll take them home and teach them love
And they'll grow up to guard my sheep.

So he picked up those baby wolves
And brought them home to show his wife.
They're wolves! she screamed. *Of course,* said he,
We'll train them in the shepherd's life.

But when they grew and ran out free,
He'd always find some poor sheep dead,
And thus he learned it's seldom wise
To let your heart defeat your head.

Moral: **Too soft a heart can**
lead to disaster.

PRAYER to find a wise spirituality

In your view, most awesome Mystery,
how clownish must seem even your most enlightened devotees.
Gifted mystics and pedestrian seekers alike:
How fragile are our spiritual skills!
Our spiritualities quickly slide off into narcissism,
wishful thinking and hankering for magic.
Instinctively grandiose and superficial at times,
we easily become complicit with half truths and false gurus,
having too soft a heart,
envying people rich where we are poor,
neglecting the solidarity with the oppressed
that alone can make our lives effective.
Build in us instead an admiration for honesty and the real,
and remove the sentimentality
that dilutes the strength of what we might do.
Amen.

Praying Your Story

Can you recall some ambition of yours that luckily did not come
about? Have you ever been too quick to help someone in need?
Have you ever been duped? Can God heal the memory?

Too soft a heart can lead to disaster.

PRAYER to John Lord Acton, English statesman

. . . to accept temporary defeats

We should not forget you, good Brother John
(but never the humble brother in life),
for your vocal objections to clerical power,
to ecclesiastical extravagances
and to all religious authoritarianism.
Your memory helps us endure such ironies in our own time
and even within ourselves.
Your refusal to be sentimental about churchmen
was a stunning witness to the depth of your faith.
Though you opposed hierarchical arrogance to the end,
you found a diplomatic if unsentimental way to compromise —
but not until you had paid the high price
of giving up your power as a public figure in the church.
We admire you the more, Lord Acton,
now that we feel comradeship with you
in the beautiful commonality of the communion of saints.
Amen.

Power tends to corrupt, and absolute power corrupts absolutely.
—Lord Acton

Biographical Note

A Life of Power and Defeat John Lord Acton (1834–1902) was an important English statesman and historian at the time of the first Vatican Council. He found himself at odds with the Pope at the time, and a critic of the church's secular power and wealth, but maintained his devotion to Christianity and Catholicism throughout his life. His final doctrinal challenge was to the teaching on papal infallibility, but he finally submitted with diplomatic ambiguity.

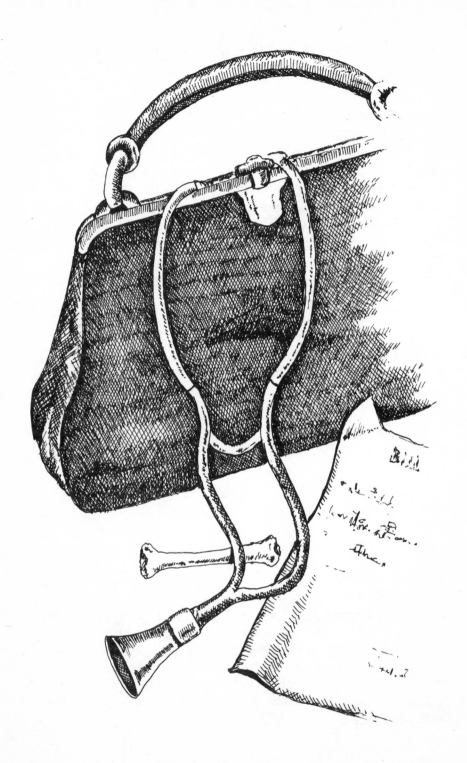

29. The Wolf Refuses To Pay His Fee

A wolf got a chicken bone stuck in his throat
And looked everywhere for relief,
Then finally sought out a heron physician
And told her the cause of his grief.

> *Well, with my long beak I can reach pretty far,*
> *For a fee I will do what I can!*
> *Okay,* said the wolf, and he opened his mouth,
> And emergency treatment began.

The heron saw teeth that were vicious and long
And a gullet revoltingly iffy,
But putting her head right into his mouth,
She plucked out that bone in a jiffy.

> *HOORAY!* said the wolf. *Two bucks!* said the bird,
> *Oh, sorry!* that heartless wolf said,
> *I won't pay the fee! Your reward is the fact*
> *That I didn't bite off your head.*

***Moral:* Never trust the powerful
to keep a promise.**

PRAYER not to judge others

Teach us, Guiding Spirit, to accept the harsh edges of life as they are
without setting up camp on the high moral ground.
Only you, Sovereign Intelligence, know our names.
You alone know what we were born to do,
have the calling to do
and are empowered to do.
You also remember perfectly all our inborn limitations,
our woundedness and our inabilities.
When it comes to other people,
we know not at all what you may expect of them,
how much freedom is at their command
and what is the final trajectory of their life.
Our attempts at moral judgments therefore —
of ourselves or others —
are foolish.
Make us wise in withholding judgment,
as prophetic voices have counseled:
"Judge not lest you be judged."
Amen.

Praying Your Story

Have you judged others too harshly? Too generously? Are you able
to withhold judgment entirely? As God sees the world, are people
too trusting or too suspicious?

Never trust the powerful to keep a promise.

PRAYER to Margaret of Scotland, saintly queen

. . . for trust despite setbacks

Extraordinary woman, Margaret, once Queen of Scotland,
dwelling now in the land where everyone is royalty,
you knew from the Gospel
that God's heart cared first for the most needy —
so each night
you invited a dozen of society's outcasts to dine at your royal table.
You did good without hope of reward,
and even at the risk of exploitation,
yet you persevered,
going forward in faith,
a heroic departure from conventional expectations.
The poor — who instinctively and wisely distrust the rich —
learned to trust you, so transparent was your caringness,
so absent was any mode of domination from your demeanor.
You inspire us.
We befriend your memory
and pray for the empowerment of a similar enlightened compassion.
Amen.

*So thoroughly did her outward bearing correspond with the firmness
of her character that it seemed as if she had been born the very pattern
of the virtuous life.*

—John Turgot

Biographical Note

A Story of a Clear-Eyed Woman Margaret's noble family was
driven out of England by the Normans in 1066, and she took refuge in nearby
Scotland where she subsequently married the king. He reverenced her for her
piety, while her deep spirituality was eloquently praised by the authoritative
monk-writer John Turgot. She cared especially for the poor, and worked hard to
guarantee the peace of her realm. She lived from 1046 to 1093, much loved by
her people, and was canonized publicly as a saint in 1250.

30. A Wily Fox Has a Hare for Dinner

A rabbit who was quite naive
Once picked a fox to be his friend.
BEWARE! warned Owl, but rabbit thought
The fox his evil ways would mend.

> *You're known for tricks!* the rabbit said
> One day as fox lay in the sun.
> *Would you be good enough, kind sir,*
> *To take the time to show me one?*

Of course, said fox, *Come by tonight*
For dinner and I'll demonstrate
How I can make things disappear
As if they just . . . evaporate!

> So that same evening fox put on
> A dinner show for his review,
> And rabbit was, to his surprise,
> Both audience and dinner too.

Moral: **The tricky can never
be trusted.**

PRAYER to be less naive

It is not because I forget about danger, my God,
that I can go forward in the dark.
It is not because I am insensitive to pain
or unfamiliar with evil in the world.
It is rather because I have no choice:
I am made for the future, my heart will be at home only there,
in the dark, in the unknown.
Something in me convinces my bones they must move on today,
and tomorrow,
dragging my fearful soul and spirit behind.
Some force larger than myself is at work, and it draws me
magnetically.
It would be naive to hold back,
to opt for isolation when true destiny appears.
I suspect, I hope, it is you,
unimaginable God in whom we live and move
and find our home.
Amen.

Praying Your Story

Do you remember ever being foolishly naive? Or have you ever tricked people yourself? Are you willing, with God's help, to repair any wrong you've done?

The tricky can never be trusted.

PRAYER to Chief Seattle, Native American hero

. . . to be trusting but wise

Be our guide today, great leader and mystic, Chief Seattle.
We model on you
our own dreams for a new kinship with earth, air and water.
You saved your people from extinction but not from heartbreak,
facing a predatory and deceitful white culture
that has since seriously degraded our common planet-home.
Now that we have learned your sublime earth-friendly ways,
it is distressing to see in perspective
the misguided mindset of many white settlers,
some of whose great sacrifices for the sake of religion were in vain.
Had they listened to you Native Americans,
they themselves may have learned
that the Holy Spirit could be found at work in your native religions,
and that "to harm the earth is to heap contempt on its creator,"
your prophetic words that fell on deaf ears.
Be our guide back to reverence for other religions,
and for our planet and its irreplaceable web of life.
Amen.

The earth is our brother; we are but one strand in the web of life;
whatever we do to that web, we do to ourselves.

—Chief Seattle

Biographical Note
———————

A Life of Disappointment and Defeat   Chief Seattle (1786?–
1866), leader of the Suquamish Indians, was chosen to lead his people in his
early twenties, a man of outstanding gifts and mystical qualities. His hopes of
living at peace with America's white settlers were dashed again and again,
and finally it was Seattle who negotiated the final compromises that led to
Indian reservations. He died on the Port Madison Reservation near the city
that bears his name.

31. A Brash Gnat Loses His Life

There once was a gnat as brash as could be
Who challenged a lion far larger than he
      To fight him and test
      Which of them was best —
Then blew on his horn and attacked like a bee.

He flew in his nostrils and buzzed in his ears,
He stung both his eyelids, which brought him to tears,
      Poor lion would claw
      His own face with his paw!
But the gnat flew away without trouble or fears.

A victory for me! sang the gnat feeling proud
While he blew on his bugle and challenged the crowd.
      But before any fought him
      A spider's web caught him,
And no one could help — though he cried very loud:

      How foolish it was for a gnat to be tryin'
      To gain a dumb victory over a lion!
One minute, I'm winner,
Then next, spider's dinner!
      Believe me, there's nothin' quite so MORTIFYIN'!

***Moral:* Often size is not decisive in conflict.**

PRAYER against expecting too much protection from God

I do not know your name, Holy One,
but I know it isn't "God."
Here our arrogance can mislead,
and modest honesty is the best guide.
Jesus instructed us to call you "Father who art in heaven."
Mohammed instructed people to call you "Allah the all merciful."
"Vishnu" seems to be your name for Hindus, one of a thousand names.
Orthodox Jews will not write or speak your name at all
though they have one.
So you have evaded identification:
How can you expect us to trust you?
You constantly disappoint our instinctive philosophizing:
unwilling or unable to protect our children from danger,
hiding when we need you most,
pretending not to exist when we seek you even under a microscope
or call out in anguish.
On the other hand, you know *our* name
and keep count of the hairs on our heads.
Is that not enough?
You entrust us with your mysteriousness.
Perhaps that is more honor than we could expect.
We give thanks.
Amen.

Praying Your Story

What might St. Paul mean by "strength made perfect in weakness"?
Have you experienced failure that was somehow a good thing?
Does God always stand by us?

Often size is not decisive in conflict.

PRAYER to John Henry Newman, Victorian Churchman

. . . for patience in seeking God

Holy creative soul, John Henry Newman,
battered scholar and fearless heart,
we find in the blaze of your courage and eloquence
heart-warming encouragement
for ourselves to follow our conscience, as you did,
wherever it may lead,
surrendering — even in our faith journey —
to the paradigm of death and resurrection,
to hope for religion even when all seems lost.
While your life was full of controversy and disappointment,
your efforts to deal with it created written lessons for us all,
and for this we — and history — are forever grateful to you.
Amen.

Lead, Kindly Light, amid the encircling gloom.
—John Henry Newman

Biographical Note

A Life of Searching and Scholarship   One of the greatest theologians, writers and thinkers of the nineteenth century, John Henry Newman's conversion to the Roman Catholic communion in 1845 rocked all England and the whole religious world. He became a priest of the Oratory, and worked for years on founding a Catholic university in Ireland, producing in the process perhaps his greatest book, *The Idea of a University*. His life was crowned with the honor of the Cardinalate at the age of seventy-eight (1801–1890).

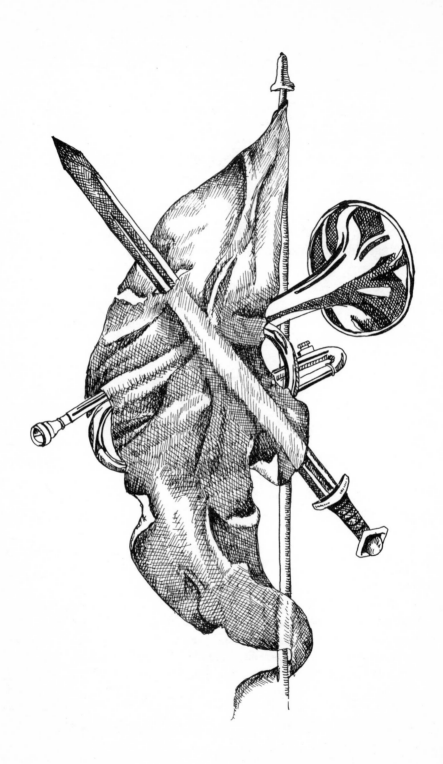

32. The Enemy's Trumpeter Is Condemned

The enemy attacked the town
And burned the barns and houses down.
> Then town folk won it back again —
> And also captured many men.

A trumpeter was in that pack
Whose stirring horn brought on the attack,
> But he demanded he go free
> Since neither knife nor sword had he.

You were the WORST of all of them,
They said: It's you we most condemn!
Although you didn't seem to fight,
You stirred their savage appetite.

> *You claim your hands gave no offense?*
> *But you urged hearts to violence!*
For music's power is passing great
To move the heart to love or hate.

> *Moral:* **Those who stir others**
> **to evil are the worst.**

PRAYER to do no harm

If we care about our spiritual life, Mysterious God,
of course we need constant guidance along its path —
for the way of wisdom can be treacherous.
False prophets and professors abound.
Illusory footbridges entice us near cavernous crevasses,
and ambition prods us forward where angels fear to tread.
With your kindly light leading, we can safely move ahead,
and if we ever guide others, we warn them first of our own mystification.
Only a few imperatives seem certain:
that we must do justice, love kindness and walk humbly with our God —
and do no harm.
Beyond that, only the foolish claim certainty.
Our own life choices necessarily model for others, trumpet for others,
our beliefs.
Give us a still mind and a focused heart.
So empowered, we can find rewarding work each day,
and a safe haven when day is done.
Amen.

Praying Your Story

What is the most dangerous type of person in your opinion? What threats to life are the most worrisome? Have you encountered evil? Can communion with God help here?

Those who stir others to evil are the worst.

PRAYER to John of the Cross, poet and reformer

. . . for spiritual wisdom

Little Brother John,
barely five feet tall, but a towering genius of intelligence, desire and poetry,
the power of your word-music extends your influence even to this day.
Be with us, modeling both human warmth and fearless prophecy,
the first perhaps inherited from your Arab mother,
the second perhaps a gift from your Jewish father's tradition.
Companion us in living passionately and prophetically,
wary of both egotistical delusion and the traps of an inert tradition.
You were the personal choice of the great Teresa of Avila
for a spiritual consultant:
Be ours also in pursuing genuine honesty with ourselves
and a wise modesty in claiming spiritual discernment.
Amen.

Where there is no love, put love, and you will draw out love.
                                        —John of the Cross

Biographical Note
_____

The Story of a Passionate Life In sixteenth century Spain, this
diminutive Carmelite priest named John of the Cross (1542–1591) managed to
have a far-reaching effect on church reform through his contacts with Teresa
of Avila. She recognized his rare gift of wisdom, and made him spiritual
director of her convent. He suffered greatly at the hands of arrogant churchmen,
barely escaping with his life. His written poetry of mysticism is considered
classical in Spanish. The church eventually made him a canonized saint and
honored him with the title Doctor of the Church.

Part V

The Wise Avoid
Foolish Expectations

33. A Tortoise Dies Trying To Fly

A tortoise once called to an eagle flying by,
Hey, what would you charge to teach me to fly?
And the eagle looked down with a groan and frowned:
Little friend, you were made to stay on the ground!

    Baloney! said the tortoise as the eagle landed near.
    You're the most selfish eagle anywhere around here!
    You act high and mighty with the tricks you know,
    And you don't care at all for the creatures below.

OK, eagle said. *Here, I'll grab your leg*
And I'll teach you to fly if you just won't beg!
So the eagle grabbed the tortoise and shot up high
Like a bright flying star in the midnight sky.

    Then he loosened his grip and the tortoise plunged down
    And SCHMUSHED like a fritter when he hit the ground.
    Then that eagle sang out in the tone of a saint:
    Only terrible fools try to be what they ain't.

Moral: **The wise avoid foolish expectations.**

PRAYER to value my inadequacies

Holy unimaginable Mystery,
if we are made in your image (whatever that may mean),
then of course you must be in some ways a failure,
so full of imperfection are we.
Do our inadequacies somehow reflect your own?
For would not an adequate God be almighty?
Yet, are you?
When we pray, even in the most desperate need,
even from the most deserving hearts,
you seem unable to help.
Mothers and children being led to massacre,
hospitals for the most deserving poor destroyed in earthquakes,
asteroids spinning through space
that could destroy every life on earth in minutes:
You do not save us from these.
Some explain you can do only what love can do:
care —
and inspire caringness —
then you suffer all our distress along with us.
We live in darkness about all this, Holy Mystery.
Enlighten us for the journey forward
for our desires (foolishly?) go beyond what we know.
Amen.

Praying Your Story

If we are to pray sensibly, what image of God is best? Does God
seem like a heavenly father to you, or like a mother? Like a wind,
or like a nothing, an illusion? Why is God so elusive?

The wise avoid foolish expectations.

PRAYER to the apostle Peter and his spouse

. . . to treasure our links with others

Holy Friends, beloved couple,
favorites of Jesus and dear to the whole circle of the Twelve —
who still, with Messiah and his mother,
celebrate together in communion with all saints and living spirits,
in the glory of the reign of God begun by Jesus' sojourn on earth —
we greet you both in prayer.
Peter, plainspoken fisherman, first Father of the church, prince of blunderers,
and you, dear Spouse with a name lost and forgotten these 2000 years
(so unimportant were you thought to be),
standing together in ministry at history's door,
you model the blessing that is community,
the strength in companionship and the spiritual revelation that is human love.
Your union hints at a key question: Is not the sacrament that is mutuality
the only force that can make a community all we can be?
Accompany us in all we do as disciples and companions of Jesus,
struggling with the incomprehensible mysteries of our world,
in faithful service to a Gospel of liberation,
a ministry of servant leadership and a community of gender equality.
Amen.

Lord, to whom shall we go? Thou hast the words of eternal life.
                    —Saint Peter, John 7: 68

Biographical Note

A Story of Denial and Bungling   The original name of Peter was
the Hebrew name Simon. Jesus renamed him "the rock," using the masculine
form of the Greek noun *petra*, rock, himself to be the church's foundation. Peter's
father was named John and their home was Bethsaida, a small fishing town in the
Galilee valley. Presumably his spouse was from the same area, and their arranged
betrothal would have occurred in childhood. He was the brother of the apostle
Andrew. They were fishermen and together were called to be disciples of Jesus.
Peter — famous in the Gospels for his bungling good will and his cowardly denial
of Jesus — became leader of the apostles, and apparently died a heroic martyr in
Rome. Two of his letters appear in the Christian Scriptures. All information
about his life companion is unrecorded except that Jesus once healed her mother.

34. A Doomed Man Enjoys Revenge

Two bitter foes got on a ship.
One sat back in the stern,
The other took a seat in front,
Annoyed and taciturn.

> Then one great wave crashed on the ship
> And filled it to the brink,
> And soon there was no doubt at all
> That little ship would sink.

The foe in back called to the mate;
Which end will go down first?
The front, my friend, the mate replied,
That's where our load is worst.

> *HURRAH!* the man in back called out,
> *Today I'm filled with glee,*
> *Knowing my foe is sure to die*
> *(Though just ahead of me).*

Moral: **Hatred can blind us to reality.**

PRAYER for forgiveness of our enemies

We instinctively love the friendly and familiar, Holy Creator,
and our fears of the unfamiliar often scare us into blind hostility,
those times when we identify "enemies."
We prefer to build comforting surroundings,
then retreat into a shell of ambiguous convictions,
forgetting that our judgments may be totally wrong.
Those we despise may, in fact, be beautiful people,
who, not unlike ourselves, are prone to disfiguring spiritual mistakes.
Open our hearts.
Give us the wisdom to ask forgiveness for all our own personal flaws,
and the mercy to welcome into forgiveness
even our most despised enemies.
Amen.

Praying Your Story

Who are our enemies? Recall people you have disliked — hated,
perhaps — or feared. Take a moment now to wish them well if you
can. We have no way of knowing how God sees them.

Hatred can blind us to reality.

PRAYER to Sojourner Truth, slave and writer

. . . for a large, forgiving heart

Poor, illiterate Sojourner Truth,
mother of thirteen, all of them sold away into slavery,
your own back marked with beatings for speaking up,
you became one of the most influential women of your day
because of your penetrating vision of God's justice
and your eloquence in that cause —
including a wide forgiveness of enemies.
Counselor to presidents and judges who were inspired
by your mystical optimism,
we feel proud to call you sister.
Be also a counselor to us.
Fill us with hope that life is larger than we know.
With you we will believe that every day of life
is meaningful for pilgrims and sojourners like us all.
Amen.

Where did Christ come from? From God and a woman. A man had nothing to do with it.

—Sojourner Truth

Biographical Note

A Prophetess for the Voiceless   Isabella Truth (1797–1883) renamed herself when her great talents thrust her into public life and she wanted to live close to the Gospels. Born a slave, the ninth child of her mother, she became the mother of thirteen children, all sold into slavery. She saw her life as a journey in a foreign land and expected an eternal reward when she died, going home, she said, "like a shootin' star." She wrote her own life story, and the book was a powerful tool in the cause of abolition of slavery. One biographer calls her "one of the most influential women of her day, an illiterate black woman, a political activist without office, a preacher without credentials, save for her penetrating vision of God's justice."

35. The Scorpion Stings the Helpful Hawk

There once was a scorpion
>Stuck at a river

And eager to cross
>With some news to deliver.

He cried: *Will some bird*
Ferry me in his claws;
I've the soul of a saint
And a heart without flaws!

Then a hawk circled down;
>*Sir,* he cried, *Let me carry*

You over, but please don't
>*do anything scary!*

Not me, said the scorpion,
I've never sinned!
>So the hawk picked him up

>And they flew like the wind.

Then ZANG! That dumb scorpion
Stung the poor guy!
>*Why'd you do that?* hawk screamed,

>*Now we'll both have to die!*

The scorpion shrugged
>with a touch of dismay,

It'*s because I'm a scorpion.*
>*What can I say?*

***Moral:* Kindness leaves you**
vulnerable.

PRAYER to risk helping others

When we reach out to those in obvious need,
we know we are being called by you, Loving Sophia.
We are never more aware of your reality
than in the experience of salving a wound,
calming a fright, nourishing a hungering human
or sharing the load with the heavy-burdened.
It is sometimes a dangerous choice,
but every human moment is edged with danger:
Safe, solitary isolation is dangerous too, mortally so.
There is no better path than to follow your call.
Inspire us with compassion as, in your own infinite compassion,
you called us each and all out of nothingness
into the evolving web of life.
Amen.

Praying Your Story

Are you familiar with ambiguity in your moral life? Do you always feel uneasy in turning down a request for help? Recall when "reaching out" was a joy. Is it not God's joy too?

Kindness leaves you vulnerable.

PRAYER to Shiphrah and other Biblical Women of Egypt

. . . for courage in risk-taking

It is an honor to remember the names of midwives Shiphrah and Puah,
of Miriam, the daughter of Pharaoh,
and of Miriam, sister of Moses,
and all the women co-laboring with men in biblical events
but themselves mostly erased from an honoring memory.
Your companionship across the ages lives on to inspire us to believe
that each of us too has meaning and a mission,
affects history and makes a difference.
You fill us with determination to carry on our roles in the world,
however demeaning or dangerous they may be.
We then may also be erased from memory,
yet we will, like you, be honored throughout eternity
in the everlasting Communion of Saints
for our risk-taking agency in helping historic things happen.
Amen.

May the subversive power of the remembered past act like a leaven,
raising the flat dough of despair, and preparing a nourishing future.
—Elizabeth Johnson

Biographical Note

Lives of Courage and Creative Disobedience   "The king
of Egypt then spoke to the Hebrew midwives, one of whom was Shiphrah,
and the other Puah. 'When you midwives attend Hebrew women,' he said,
'watch the birth carefully. If it is a boy, kill him; if a girl, let her live.' But the
midwives were God-fearing; they disobeyed the command of the king of Egypt
and let the boys live" (Exodus 1:15-17).

36. A Wolf Finds Reasons for Eating a Lamb

A conscientious wolf one day
Saw a lamb take a drink at a stream.
Ah, what can I say to that lamb, he thought,
To explain my murderous scheme?

> *Someone has muddied the water!* cried wolf,
> *And you're the one to be blamed!*
Oh no, said lamb. *I'm not upstream!*
And I only sipped! he claimed.

> *But why did you slander my father last year,*
> Asked the wolf, *and say that he stoled?*
Oh, that wasn't poor little me, laughed the lamb,
I'm only a few months old.

> *No matter your quickness of tongue,* said wolf,
> *However you banter and kid,*
> *I'm still going to have you for LUNCH today*
> *With a side dish of greens.* And he did.

Moral: **The motives we claim
can be far from the truth.**

PRAYER for honesty

Are we capable of being candid with ourselves, O Holy Mysterious One?
Can we find, at least occasionally, courage in our hearts
to know ourselves as we are?
Our games of hide-and-seek, of oblique question and guarded response,
of thrust and dodge, are familiar
and played by most of us —
yet we have an instinct for honesty and a drive for intimacy and trust.
Alas, we often do not really know our motivations,
and can be surprised by the forthright honesty of others.
Make us our best and truest selves, ever-parenting Spirit,
for our hearts are restless for honest knowledge
and uneasy until they are fully true.
Amen.

Praying Your Story

Have you ever doubted your own motivations? Do you recall having mixed motives for something you did? Is it comforting or not to recall that God knows us perfectly?

The motives we claim can be far from the truth.

PRAYER to Edith Stein, victim of the Shoah

. . . for candid honesty

Faithful, martyred heroine, Edith Stein, devout Jew to the end,
now become a model for all who search for God,
just as you went to your death with your people at Auschwitz,
so you empower us to be faithful to our own vocation,
however unique that call may be.
You can be a reminder for us of the need for candid honesty
since — contrary to ecclesiastical claims —
it was your ethnic origins, not your Christianity,
that brought about your death.
Even that wonderfully brilliant, prodigious intelligence of yours
could not save you from hatred,
but it has enriched us all with enlightening memories of you,
and led us to learn to find comfort in a religion
that stands against and outlives
the impenetrable darkness of human evil.
Amen.

If you are serious . . . you will be present . . . at every front; at every place of sorrow, bringing to those who suffer, healing and salvation.
—Edith Stein

Biographical Note
———————

Faithful Christian, Faithful Jew   Born into an orthodox Jewish family, at age thirteen, after demonstrating a most unusual intelligence, Edith Stein (1893–1942) declared herself an atheist. She received a doctorate in Philosophy at age twenty-three. In 1921 she became a Christian and taught in a Catholic school, but she accompanied her mother weekly to the synagogue. She soon joined the Carmelite Order, but Nazi oppression reached into the convent, and Edith was forced to wear the yellow Star of David on her habit. She died in the gas chamber of Auschwitz on August 9, 1942, and was declared a saint in 1995.

37. A Stork Chooses Bad Companions

A farmer sowed a field of corn,
    But cranes soon came to call.
So he made traps to catch those cranes
    Before they ate it all.

One day he found he'd caught a stork
    Within his circling noose,
The stork cried, *Wait, I'm not a crane.*
    Kind sir, please turn me loose!

YOU FOOL! said Farmer. *Why did you*
    With cranes associate?
You chose to share their company,
    You now must share their fate.

Moral: **There is risk in expressing solidarity.**

PRAYER for the courage to love

You have set before my eyes, Creator of love and magnetism,
needy people beautiful to me,
their needs calling out to my own,
the symmetry of their continuing heroism
stunningly awesome to my heart,
their need of me a miracle of self-discovery in my own life.
My heart goes out to them, embraces them —
despite the vulnerability this creates in me.
What human has not known the cost — besides the joy —
that can come from reaching out?
Yet out we go, into the deep mystery of compassion, again and again,
reaching out to those in pain.
It is the miracle of magnetism
you have inserted in our human hearts and bodies,
a mirror image of your own.
With you, then, we rejoice in the grace of solidarity,
and pay the cost willingly.
Amen.

Praying Your Story

Think of times when you have joined in an altruistic effort involving risk. What, if anything, draws you to solidarity? Do you understand why some people prefer living in isolation?

There is risk in expressing solidarity.

PRAYER to Martin de Porres, servant of the poorest

. . . for a compassionate heart

Brother Martin, we come to you for a model of healing.
Have you a balm to heal the soul of our world?
Healer Brother and heart of compassion whom the sick so loved,
can your example and companionship empower us today
to rise above racism and despair
and to become one earthly family?
Orphan Brother to poor orphans, but beloved among the wealthy as well,
your empowering memory can heal today
as you once did in Peru 300 years ago.
Help us find a path to interracial justice and societal health
for our hurting and divided human family.
Amen.

They called him father of the poor.

—A contemporary witness

Biographical Note

A Life of Self-Giving Martin de Porres (1579–1639) was the son of a Spanish nobleman stationed in Peru and of an African mother, once a slave. He showed great talent at an early age and was accepted by the Dominican fathers as a dedicated helper and skilled healer. His compassion for the poor was prodigious and even legendary, yet he was beloved by all for his kindly manners and intelligence. Eventually he was accepted as a lay brother of the Order, and became famous throughout Peru until his death in 1639. He was canonized a saint by Pope John XXIII in 1962.

38. The Tricky Wolf Dons Sheep's Clothing

There once was a wolf as sharp as a pin
Who loved to dress in an old sheep's skin
So shepherds would not see him creep
Among the flocks of grazing sheep.

Then he would kill and eat his fill
Whenever he came up the hill
Where shepherds like to spend the day,
Safe, they thought, from danger's way.

One day the shepherd thought he'd take
The fattest mutton home to bake,
With arrow poised, his bow he bent —
And shot THAT WOLF by accident!

O, what a fool I am, wolf said,
And wept because he'd soon be dead,
*I thought my fine disguise was slick
But caught myself in my own trick.*

Moral: **Disguises can be
dangerous.**

PRAYER for help in removing disguises

How clearly you see through our pretenses, Holy Mystery.
The human imagination leads us to put on disguises occasionally,
masking pain, masking dislike,
masking ignorance, even masking — covering over — love.
We know the masks do not work for you:
You see through them all.
Remind us often of that.
And give us a style of relationship with others that is never dissembling,
always frank and unpretentious,
for we long for a world in which we need not pretend,
nor keep our hearts in hiding.
Amen.

Praying Your Story

Are there incidents in your life where you have kept your true face
hidden? Is dissembling easy or hard for you? Can God help us be
ingenuous?

Disguises can be dangerous.

PRAYER to John Howard Griffin, twentieth century author

. . . for inventive zeal

Brother John, heroic challenger of racism,
since you were gifted in your life with so-called "radical empathy,"
is it possible you can be empathetic for even the non-heroic among us?
Few can follow you in your pell-mell campaigns
to save Jews during the Shoah
(narrowly escaping with your life),
or in entering fully the U.S. racial struggle
by becoming black yourself (with drugs, dyes and radiation).
We honor you as a hero,
although the heroic is normally beyond us.
Instead we live with caution and ambiguity
in our efforts to oppose the evils in society,
feeling that is our calling from the same God
who called you more radically.
We feel your brotherly support in all we do,
radical in desire if not often in action.
Amen.

I go to live on the other side of the river, hoping to find that it is no different from this side, and that we can no longer justify demonizing people for such false reasons.
—John Howard Griffin

Biographical Note

A Life Far-Out and Fearless The incorrigible activist and author of *Black Like Me*, John Howard Griffin (1920–1980) early in life helped run a network in Europe that smuggled Jews to safety. An injury left him totally blind, but the condition cleared up after several years, and he devoted himself to writing fiction. After masquerading as a black and writing his book about it, he was burned in effigy in his hometown, and his life was threatened. For years he suffered from many illnesses and died at the age of 60, ill and worn out with his work for justice and peace.

39. A Donkey Thinks He Is Divine

A donkey once was led to town
With a statue of Zeus on his back.
When bystanders started bowing down,
He stopped and his jaw went slack.

I must be a GOD, the donkey said,
How could all these people misjudge?
So he flickered his eyes like a holy sage
And brayed, and would not budge.

The driver's whip was quick to flash,
Correcting the donkey's fault
And teaching that ass it's wise to take
All praise with a grain of salt.

Moral: **Be suspicious of too much deference.**

PRAYER to be slightly credulous

O unreachably intimate Spirit,
when I feel numb to your awesome intimacy —
so intimate to me that your mystery has become part of my own —
rouse my soul, awaken me to reality:
You are God and the source of being wherever being is.
You are totally beyond,
yet we can never be separated;
that is a fact and a consolation.
And if divinity is so intimate to myself,
then the world is necessarily numinous,
crammed with wonders.
In fact, "Nothing is too wonderful to exist," as the scientists tell us.
May I be alert to the miracles all around,
within my purview and hearing,
at my fingertips and on every side.
Be part of my life, my being and my consciousness, Holy Mystery.
Amen.

Praying Your Story

Have you been lucky in your life? Did you grow up in a family privileged in some way? Were you ever eager to join an elite? Do real elites exist in God's eyes?

Be suspicious of too much deference.

PRAYER to Anthony of Padua, famous preacher and saint

. . . in gratitude for miracles

Sweet, gifted brother Anthony,
thirteenth century "wonder worker,"
friend of the poor,
reluctant to preach until the great Francis of Assisi himself called you to it,
be a brother to us today.
Faintly we still hear the sound of that melodious voice of yours,
so inspiring to your listeners.
Many of us await a call as you did,
reluctant to take the initiative in word or deed.
While we wait, our care will be for the same poor you cared for,
to reduce their pain and humiliation,
to assure them there is hope ahead.
We know that the same Divine Mystery that cares particularly for them
stands under all the miracles that exist,
physical or spiritual.
And if the unbelievable speed of light is a constant and unfailing creation,
how much more reliable will be our Creator's promised compassion
for all the marginalized.
Wonder-worker saint, be with us.
Let us hear again your charismatic message of faith.
Amen.

O Sweet Jesus, what is there sweeter than Thee? Sweet is Thy memory,
sweeter than that of honey or any other object....
> —Anthony of Padua

Biographical Note

The Life of a Wonder-Worker   Born in Lisbon, Portugal, Saint Anthony (1195–1231) first joined the Augustinian Order, then left to become a Franciscan and evangelist. Ill health forced him to abandon his dangerous missionary activities among the Moors in Morocco. On his return voyage, his ship landed accidentally in Italy, and there he stayed, becoming famous for preaching and for his mission of healing. Anthony died on June 13, 1231, at the age of only thirty-six. He is officially a Doctor of the Church.

40. A Patient Dies of Good Symptoms

A wealthy man once felt upset
And told the doctor how he sweat
      At night upon his mat.
The doctor, eager him to please,
Told him: *Relax and take your ease,*
      A healthy symptom, that.

But soon he came again and said
Now he was shivering in his bed,
      Could hardly even breathe!
The doctor smiled: *Relax, my dear,*
It's a good symptom, do not fear,
      Soon that distress will leave.

Next diarrhea hit the man;
It's good, it shows you're eating bran,
      The foolish doctor guessed.
The man EXPIRED! His family cried:
'Twas of good symptoms that he died!
      The doctor did his best.

***Moral:* Beware of shortsighted experts.**

PRAYER of apology for mistreating the earth

Holy Parenting Spirit, Sophia-Creator,
we, your human children come to you
admitting the wrong we have done
to this precious planet-home we call earth,
for the shameful condition of our water, soil and air,
all vital to our continuing to live and thrive here.
The gracious, evolving planet-home you invented for us long ago
has its rich topsoil almost exhausted by overuse,
its gracious waters so polluted in many areas that wildlife may
no longer live there,
its web of life scarred and torn with the loss of beautiful animals and plants
now forever extinct,
its rain forests, major sources of the air we breathe, depleted and deforested,
our blanket of fresh air defiled
and our protective ozone layer dangerously thinned.
What is worse: Our destructive lifestyles are continuing,
driven by ignorance and greed for profit.
See how distressed we are:
We earthlings, ignoring far-sighted wisdom, are suffocating ourselves
and diminishing our future prospects.
Gift us at last with the wisdom of a loving caringness for Mother Earth,
a new spirit of reverence for life and for all life's earthen resources,
and passionate opposition to whatever further debases our only homeland,
the living earth.
Amen.

Praying Your Story

Recall what was the most foolish advice you ever gave? Have you ever experienced denial, refusing to know something inconvenient or uncongenial?

Beware of shortsighted experts.

PRAYER to Kateri Tekakwitha, Native American mystic

. . . for a love of nature's way

You are our companion, Holy Kateri,
as we seek honesty
and to befriend the honest earth at last,
to find the divine in the ubiquitous marvels of the natural world
and to live in harmony with living things everywhere.
The natural world is a sacrament of honesty,
admitting to the presence of the divine within it,
and knowing nothing of deception.
Help us take its warnings at face value
and work to guard its limited resources.
In your perception of the violence done by misguided colonists
against your land and against your Iroquois nation, Sister Kateri,
we perceive your own honesty,
but in your wisdom
we learn to be wise as well,
desiring never again to exploit defenseless peoples or the vulnerable earth.
Teach us to live reverently and honestly in these green fields and forests
and to make future generations at home here,
sharing the earth's abundance with generosity and caution.
Amen.

She was a lily of innocence, a flaming fire of intelligence, a fountain of joy and promise for all who knew her.
— Jesuit Relations

Biographical Note

A Life Far From Home   Daughter of a Mohawk Iroquois chief and an Algonquin mother, Kateri Tekakwitha (1656–1680) converted to Christianity, defying the traditions of her tribe. This put her life in grave danger, so, with the advice of the Jesuit missionaries, she went to live in a community in Sault St. Louis, 200 miles away. There she was revered as a saint, and became beloved for her compassion for the needy and her active life of prayer and self-sacrifice.

Epilogue: **The Fable of My Life**

William Cleary

In 1976 when you stepped up into Hopkins Bookshop, you found yourself in a tunnel-shaped space colored with earthen shades of orange and green. The prevailing smell of garlic came from the sub shop next door that was linked to us by a common basement, a dank stone-edged cave where we had our office. The upstairs was bright though, and a 40-foot mural outside carried our orange and green motif down the side-street alley.

You would have seen all this in Burlington, Vermont, in the little state's most bustling city, a bookstore located right across from City Hall, situated on the last block of a four-block "Church Street" leading up to a red brick colonial church with "1816" etched high on its clock tower.

On a good day greeting card displays would be spinning, a rabbi would be browsing among our Jewish books in the window, two nuns from one of the nearby Catholic colleges would be asking for new titles by Schillebeeckx and Rahner. My wife Roddy (a part-time campus minister at the University of Vermont, just up the hill) would be activating the clumsy ching of our brass cash register, and Yours Truly would be sitting on the steps leading up to our children's section reading the Narnia Tales to two pre-school children who clearly resembled both me and the check-out lady.

If the poet Gerard Manley Hopkins (whom we named our store after) is on target when he states that "every mortal thing deals out that being indoors dwells, selves, goes itself, proclaiming 'what I do is me,'" this whole bookstore scene is a snapshot of my "self" at age 50, in the virtual middle of a "fabulous" life. On my face one might read the intensity lines of one who had been a Jesuit for twenty-two years, who married at age forty-three, and had become the father of two challenging sons. My bride had been a Religious Sister, a Ph.D. candidate in theology at Fordham University at the time, and the kind of intellectual who could combine great common sense, an avid feminism and solidarity with the marginalized. We have been blessed as spiritual companions for thirty-two years, and when my personal fable is over and has become just another animated film in heaven, Roddy will be featured there as my life's sunshine, my soul's daily sacrament and my heart's home.

Though this book is about making sense of one's life, my essential self, my meaning, still eludes definition, fading in and out like the misty Northern Lights that sometimes shine at night in these parts. Perhaps I would call myself essentially a dreamer, a kind of foolish young farmer who assiduously planted cash crops — soy beans, alfalfa, tobacco, sugar cane — unaware that at midnight sweet Mother Demeter would come by and charm his plantings into becoming spinach, corn, melons and grapes: a salad, a main dish, a dessert and a wine — in short, a whole.

For instance, my life makes sense now despite the fact that, while I've had lots of good luck, much of what I tried to do failed. In my earliest days as a Jesuit, though no-nonsense Father Gschwend, my novice master, tried continuously to get me into the role of an Ignatius Loyola or a Francis Xavier, I secretly, compulsively, was becoming Bing Crosby. The song "Goin' My Way" still brings tears to my eyes, so important did it figure in my early subliminal motivations. I was good at singing, I could play the piano, I could act: Bing was my role model. I couldn't help myself. We both looked great in a Roman collar.

My next task was to study, and that required heroics as well, filling a total of thirteen college-level years with books, papers, dramatics, music, liturgy, languages, meditations, disputations and above all — and most sweetly — conversations. We filled in all our non-study time with talk, and that more than anything else was my most satisfactory educational experience.

Finally ordained a priest in 1960, I soon left for the Korean missions to teach English and music at Sogang University. There life became wildly exciting and satisfying: the devastated third-world country, the eager friendly students, music to create, the language to learn, our own church renewal of Vatican Council II, teaching, traveling, writing: my first book accepted by a New York publisher.

All this came to an end in 1966 when my dream of an agency for Jesuit writers in New York City was handed over to me to implement. It took several years and lots of travel. In 1968, once my Writers Agency task was done and given to others, instead of returning to Korea, a Jesuit friend and I dreamed up a movie company, creating short discussion films for use in our American schools. The company floundered at first and then succeeded, and exists to this day though both the founders have long ago left the Jesuit Order.

In 1972, now the father of two, I took a managerial job in a Washington, DC, bookstore, and three years later (after the store was held up five times) started my own in Vermont. The world of religious books enabled my wife and me to remain up-to-date in theology and spirituality, not to mention being acquainted with the new music that was coming alive within institutional Christianity — to which I dreamed of contributing.

My dreamer-self continued to plant cash crops. During the Sandinista Revolution in Nicaragua in the early 80s, three outstanding Catholic priests were given key governmental posts there — Foreign Minister, Minister of Culture and Minister of Education — and I dreamed up a whimsical song, then a 15-minute video, entitled *Padre Ernesto*. The song dramatized the work of these priests and the great ideals of that ill-fated revolution. I thought my music could satisfy my need to contribute to the cause, but no such luck. People around me (my wife, for instance) were spending weeks and weeks in that Central American country, helping bring its idealistic dream to life. I found myself sucked into a cotton-picking brigade, and in no time, I was flying south at the risk of my life.

I survived — barely — the heat and rodents of that work, but as I settled into my seat in an American Airlines plane jetting out of Miami after just two weeks picking cotton, I could not have been more exultant. Not only was I still alive, but three promising stars sparkled in my professional sky: my politico/religious song group had a Cleary-music gig in Los Angeles, opening for Judy Collins; I had a contract for a song album with the biggest religious music publisher in the U.S.; and the Asia Society had agreed verbally to stage my Korean musical off-off Broadway. "Each mortal thing does one thing and the same: deals out that being indoors each one dwells, selves ...." I felt at that moment that I was about to deal out my truest being, about to *selve* grandiloquently.

None of it happened. Over the next months each star fell from my sky in its own melancholy way. Why was this happening, I asked myself, unaware that sweet Demeter was continuing her wily work.

For a full-figured dreamer like myself, it was this pattern of sobering disappointment that became a theme in my work life. My campaign song for candidate Geraldine Ferraro which cost thousands of dollars to make and six months to promote, got nowhere. My anti-drug film "Everybody's Goin' Where I've Been" went nowhere also, even after the U.S. Army said they loved it and began talking of a six-figure purchase. The campaigns to prevent aid to the Contras, to forestall the Iraqi War, to aid the passing of the Equal Rights Amendment, all failed. Even Cliff Robertson's voice could not make a hit out of a little anti-war film *Holy War*. My long novel about Korea did not impress some thirty publishers. Despite all this, I have to admit to many charmed outcomes — especially in the lovable personal warmth and jazz inventions of pianist son Tom, and in the passionate and downhome compositions of singer/songwriter son Neil. They remind me daily of the sweet fable of my life, the inept farmer surreptitiously assisted by heaven.

In the great scheme of things, my personal niche of belonging is modest, I believe. Bill Cleary belongs to that scheme mainly due to his active streak of inventiveness. The products of my creativity have not been world-shaking ideas or stratospheric spiritual leadership, but most often just an elaboration on the philosophy and religion that have made up my ever-changing spirituality. Here my chief claim has to do with what is called "prayer" — but that includes for me every kind of approach to the Divine Mystery itself, speaking into its silence, trying to feel comfortable with its darkness. My first book (*Facing God*, written in Korea) elaborated twenty different ways to spend time in meditation (I was finding it hard to do). My second book (*Hyphenated Priests*) predicted an end to professional "priests" who had no other profession but ministry; the book gave lifestyle accounts of a dozen priest-professionals — thus "hyphenated" — priest-lawyers, priest-professors, priest-scholars.

Next I became a hyphenated priest myself, a priest-filmmaker. I worked on just four films at that time, but one of them (*Me and the Monsters*) luckily hit just the right note for public schools, and has been used by them for twenty-seven years. If I have made any significant mark on my milieu, it is through this 10-minute children's film on fear. At the time I made it, my personal life was changing dramatically as I was taking on a secular lifestyle. After I lost confidence in filmmaking (not knowing how successful it would eventually be), I began bookselling, a profession that occupied me for fifteen years.

When we finally sold our store in 1985, I began to write and compose full time. Since then publishers of spiritual books, musical tapes and faith development videos have found my whimsical products coming through their transoms, and some have been gracious enough to publish them. *Praying Your Story* has helped me look positively on it all and hope for the best. May it help you do the same.

So the naive farmer continued to plant seeds of many kinds: but only heaven can — and will — make sense of it. For many another human perhaps that has to be life's only appraisal, penultimate but hope-filled.

Nowadays, at age 75, I labor on — with projects always awaiting attention in my studio of dreams, a computer program called "workroom." I am in there every day, eagerly *selving* away. Still, once a month, at the Burlington Health and Rehabilitation Center, with fifteen wheelchairs pulled up around my top-opened piano and my uncertain Irish tenor singing out "I'll Take You Home Again, Kathleen" or even "The Bells of St. Mary's" with other quavering voices all coming alive around me, Father Time gets stopped in his tracks and whisked back 50, 60 or 70 years, I feel at that moment that my life is fabulous. I have almost become the Bing Crosby of my dreams, though now no longer dressed like Father O'Malley. It seems that, for the musical time-outside-of-time, trouble and pain all forgotten, memories are awakening again filled with romantic dreams still alive in the land where anything's possible.

Index of Saints